OUT OF THE BOX

THE FULL STORY

LEROY SMITH
JAMES SEYMOUR

Out of the Box: The Full Story
Second Edition published 2020
Originally published 2016
OUTOFTHEBOXBOOK Publisher Limited
www.outoftheboxbook.uk
outoftheboxbook@outlook.com

A catalogue record is available for this book from the British Library
ISBN 978-0-9955520-4-3
Designed and typeset by James Waters (www.jamespwaters.com)

Double Cat A

Extremely dangerous

New Scotland Yard

Reference #5 S

Mr BARTON P.M.S.

LEEROY SMITH.

I have today attended an assem[bly] meeting at N.S.Y. in relation to the above named. Smith is currently imprisoned in the U.S.A. and is wanted for the shooting of two police officers in Brixton in March 1994. The circumstances of this offence are that two unarmed officers went to stop a motorcycle on a routine check. The motorcycle was being driven by Parchment (Cat A standard risk at Bellmarsh) Smith was the pillion passenger. As one of the officers approached the vehicle Smith withdrew a handgun and shot the officer at point blank range, then turned on the other officer and shot him. Both officers were seriously wounded and Smith made good his escape.

Smith was at that time on the run from an escape from escort. During the escort in a taxi Smith produced a knife and threatened escorting officers and gained his freedom. It is suspected that while on the run Smith was responsible for five other shootings and several armed robberies. He is described by the officer leading the investigation

00011/6

as a top class robber who is totally ruthless. Some of the robberies that Smith is suspected of were done on his own and others were comitted by a gang of 3 or 4.

After the Brixton shooting Smith escaped to America where he began a drugs business, importing drugs into the U.K. He took with him a group of five women from the U.K to act as couriers. He suspected one woman of trying to cheat him so he went with a second woman to an isolated location and shot her. (The purpose of taking the second woman with them was to display to her what might happen if she attempted to cheat Smith). He was subsequently arrested for this offence and is held in a New York prison.

Reference PDP/S.32396/5/4.

Charged as follows

Attempt murder of 2 police officers
Attempt murder of unknown person.
Escape lawful custody
Assault prison officer
Firearms offences
Armed Robbery x3.

Miss Hughes PMS.

I have today attended an assesment meeting at N.S.Y. regarding the production of Smith to Kilburn ID suite at 2.30p on Monday 1st August 1994. It was decided at the meeting that an armed escort would be provided for Smiths production and that there would be an armed presence at the ID suite.

Ken Dec
Asst. Police Adviser
21.7.94.

Issue MO
27.7.94

27/7/94

Mo faxed & sent
27.7.94.

T/c to Belmarsh Security. Smith is not to be charged with any further offences following I/D parade

5/8/94

000119

No. 402A

METROPOLITAN POLICE

Division ZU

Station Parchmore Road

26th January 1995

For the information of the

Antecedents of: (show full name) Leroy Martin SMITH

Committed for trial/~~sentence~~ at Central Criminal Court

For offences of (1) Attempted Murder of James SEYMOUR
(2) Attempted Murder of Simon CARROLL
~~(3) Attempted Murder of Whitfield GRIFFITHS~~
(4) Armed Robbery
(5) Possession of Firearm with Intent to Endanger Life X 2
(6) GBH with Intent X 3

Date and Place of birth

[redacted] London.

Age 26

Date of first entry into U.K. N/A

Nationality British

Date of arrest 01.07.94

In custody/~~On bail~~

Brief summary of convictions

Theft - 7.3.83
Theft - 12.12.83
Burglary - 21.12.83
Burglary, Theft, Handling, Assault, Theft Person - 10.6.85
Robbery X 2 - 21.10.85
Burglary - 25.11.85
Theft - 20.8.83
Theft - 9.2.88
Offensive Weapon - 8.1.88
Offensive Weapon - 19.12.85
Theft from Person - 21.10.8
Blackmail - 21.10.87
Offensive Weapon - 7.7.89

Education:

Educated at Henry Thornton Primary School, Left aged 13

~~Main employments since leaving school: (Include details of any military service etc.)~~

[redacted]

Contents

Foreword

Freeze Motherfucker!

'Don't move! Don't move! I've got you motherfucker! I'm going to blow your head off!'

That was the moment when time stopped for me. Here I was in 1994, 25 years' old and being arrested by a FBI SWAT team in Connecticut, USA. The game and the party were over.

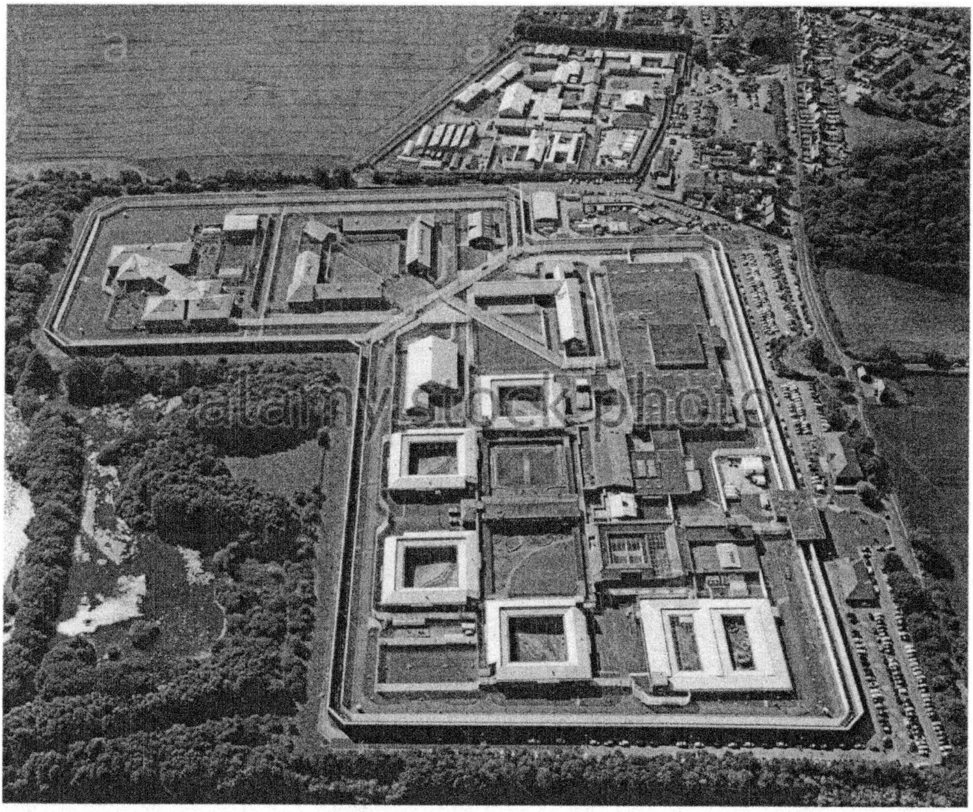

Frankland prison

Chapter 1

Early life

Hello. My name is Leroy Smith. I was a 1960s' baby. I was born on 5 November 1968 in St Thomas's Hospital and I was brought up by my grandmother, Gladys, in Clapham, South London. My mother Perlita was murdered when I was two years' old. My earliest memory was, as a two-year-old, seeing my mother in that wooden box with the glass top. I didn't understand what it meant at the time, but even at that age, I knew that something wasn't right. In hindsight it probably was not the best place to have taken me and I feel it may have shaped my future in some way.

My earliest memories of school were flying. I had a friend, Roy White. He was my best friend and we did not notice that we were not the same colour; we were just happy to play games and read together. One day we were told to make flags because the Queen was coming past the school for us to wave at her, and we were all very happy to make the flags. When the day finally came, we all stood and waved the flags we'd made as she drove past in her Rolls-Royce. Life seemed fun.

It was at Christmas a year or two later that I first saw the drama called Roots, which is all about the evil atrocities of the slave trade. That was my first introduction to the real world where black was more than just a colour. This reality had a profound effect on me and planted the mindset that would influence my future.

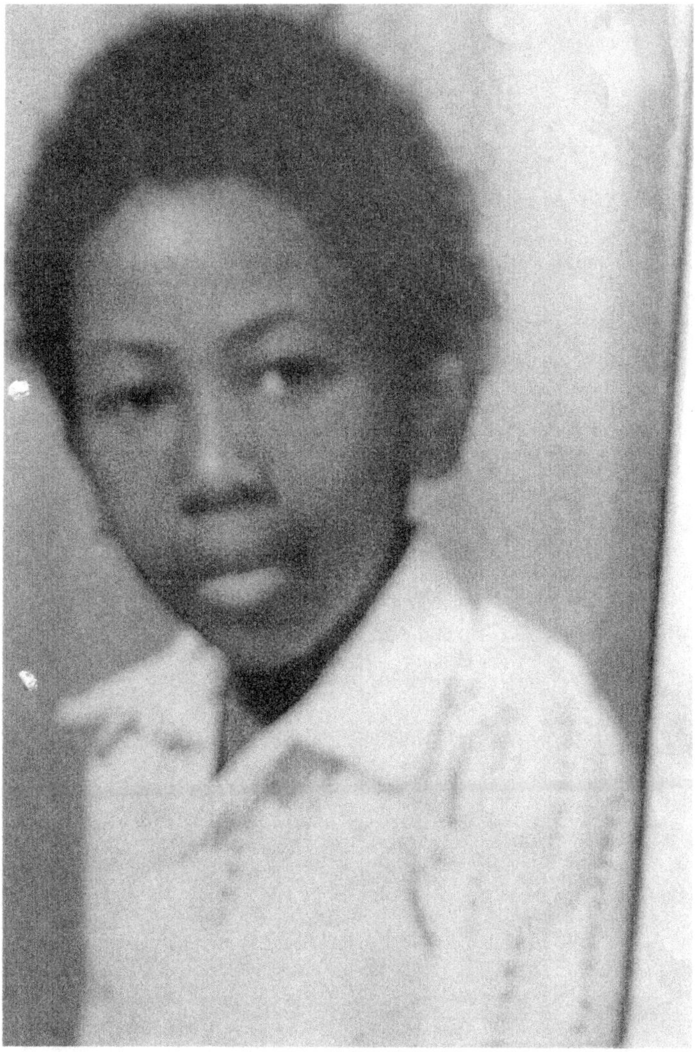

Chapter 2

Juvenile crime

Once I got to about 12 years old, I stopped going to school and started bunking off, smoking weed with my little friends from the flats in the council estate where I grew up. At that time in the 1980s there were lots of colourful characters around, older guys that we could look at as role models, and, to be honest, the ones that seemed to have the most of everything were armed robbers or those generally dealing with violent crime. Back in those days the violence was minimal - somebody would do an armed robbery with maybe just a knife, or pretend to have a gun, and still get away with it. It was a time of hot summers and fun but this was also the time when I had my first introduction to the Metropolitan Police.

I was 12 years old and had stolen a camera from somebody who had visited my house. The police were called and they decided in their wisdom to take me into the kitchen on my own and give me a good talking to. This just happened to be a little while after seeing that programme I referred to earlier called Roots. The two did not go down very well together and I remember feeling a form of resentment towards them, because it seemed like they were telling me that in a few years' time they were going to enjoy locking me up.

In this period from 12 years old to 15 years old, I started hanging around with one of my cousins who lived in Vauxhall. Vauxhall is a few miles from where I lived in Clapham. He had a few friends, so we ended up being a young little gang for want of a better word. We used to smoke cannabis and break into shops and houses and steal from cars in places like Pimlico and Victoria, which are rich hubs for the city, with a high volume of wealthy people passing through every day.

By then, I'd also learned to drive. I remember I was 13 years old and one of our group had stolen a Morris Minor and he was revving it, trying to drive it, and I was standing there with some of our girls and my cousin, and I decided that I could drive it. So I got in and somebody put the handbrake down and we were off. We drove all around South London, choking and spluttering, revving along the way. You couldn't make it up. The next morning, I drove the car right into the back of a bus by accident and from that day on I classed myself as someone who could drive! That's the way it was. Everything was just happening, slowly sliding into a free-for-all that was dictated, even then, by the need for money or the chance to make some, no matter how small the amount.

This urge for money pushed me further down the wrong path, and further away from the road chosen by most people. In hindsight that is the best way to explain it.

I did still have a father who had now moved on and got himself a new partner and was in the process of making a new family for himself and he did try to get custody of me from my grandparents, but by that stage it was already too late.

My immediate family who I lived with - my mother's brothers and sisters - were all law-abiding citizens, apart from one who was always in and out of prison. He was just like a shady character on the outskirts, while everybody else was law-abiding. One of my uncles was also in the army for a short while, so I did not have any real reason inside my household to explain what kept pulling me towards the side of life that at the time I knew nothing about.

Chapter 3
Borstal

I carried on in this vein and became more and more detached from school and the normal things that young people my age would be doing. It did not take long for me to start getting into more problems with the police, all kinds of things ranging from theft to burglary. In the end I was sentenced to four months in Send young offenders' institute in Surrey.

When you are 14 years old, four months sounds and feels like forever. It was a very, very hostile and nasty place and the staff took joy in being sadistic to the inmates. Your daily routine would be breakfast in the morning, which consisted of porridge and a pasty round object which the lads had decided to call a brick, and which they used as a countdown for how many days to their release; for example, five days left is four days and a brick. Then, after breakfast, we'd parade on the exercise yard like miniature soldiers and stand to attention. Then you would have to go to the gym, where they trained you until you drop, and if you did drop they would call you a sissy, screaming at you 'see, you never cared about your mum when you were grabbing them handbags'. Sometimes as a punishment we would have to clean the corridor with a toothbrush. This corridor ran from one end of the prison to the other. After the gym there was work, which consisted of picking strawberries or other fruit, or clearing stinging nettles from the ground in order to plant new fruits. This was all done with bare hands. That place would make or break any child and I don't believe that the public would believe that these things actually did go on.

There was a nightman called Chips and if one person was talking at night, he'd get the whole dormitory out of bed and make them unfold and refold their bedpacks. Then he'd call some boys to the bars and pull their hair so their heads hit against the bars, going on about how we were all scum. All this courtesy of Her Majesty.

I did my three out of four months there and came out a lot physically stronger. Life at that time just seemed like fun, with no real comprehension of time or future, just living for the here and now. I started getting girlfriends of my age, or maybe a little bit older, and we and other young lads of my age started going out on day trips to explore. We ended up in places like Surrey and Hampshire. That's when I really started to understand or notice how some people live; it was surprising to me, it really was and eventually we started going to those places looking for opportunities to make money. By that stage my moral compass was formed and I did not have an issue with taking every opportunity I could. I didn't have a master plan to save money and buy a house or things which people normally aspire to or think about. I only wanted money to live, and so I could have and do whatever I perceived to be fun. We were still kids and only wanted to smoke weed and try our luck around girls.

One of the many times as a juvenile that I ended up inside the penal system, I was put on remand in Brixton prison. That prison was for adults but they had been putting juveniles in there due to lack of spaces for juveniles in certain parts of the country. Anyway, I ended up in Brixton in a cell with another young lad who turned out to live in my estate. I will just call him Steve - a mixed race lad, very, very smart for a young person at the time; we clicked straight away and so our friendship started. We linked up again on the outside and then just started exploring the countryside all over: Surrey, Windsor, Oxfordshire, Buckinghamshire, and we soon learned how to benefit from the elements, i.e. winter, for what we were doing.

Chapter 4

Rise to infamy

I remember these times as fun. Well, what I knew to be fun then, especially as I always had money, even though looking back now, that was the road that was going to lead me ultimately to disaster and none of the proceeds on my part really did anything positive for me. I was young and my impression of the world was already tainted; therefore on reflection. I would have to say that by this stage, I was more interested in ways of getting whatever I wanted for me and whoever I classed as my friends.

In England, there are only a handful of ways that someone could have a firearm. One is to get a licence. These are mostly given to middle class Caucasian English men who tend to live in places like Surrey, Windsor and Oxfordshire. Therefore, it was only a matter of time, if you were a burglar, until you would come across a firearm. These were in the form of a shotgun or a pump action rifle, which is the same thing, basically, although the mechanism is different, giving it the ability to hold cartridges and therefore hold five or six rounds instead of a shotgun's two.

It was at this stage that you put all your options on the table and decide what you are going to do. So, we decided that we would keep the first one we found, and eventually, in the course of one of our burglaries, we did indeed come across a shotgun. Steve, being a person who loved fixing and pulling things apart, decided that he would cut the barrel to effectively turn it into a sawn-off. There was no real reason to have it at that stage, but we kept it and occasionally I would go and get it. On one occasion I pulled it on somebody as a joke and I was totally surprised at the fear in the person and the power that I felt.

This was a turning point in my mindset, because it led me to start understanding that, in the community that I was living in, a lot of the people that seemed scary were not really scary after all. Once you had that gun in your hand, the mindset and momentum just built from there and the more I started using it and doing things, then being dead quiet in public, the more people seemed to be scared of me. This can be a good or a bad thing. If you are nice when you get what you want, but people know you are capable, it puts you in a position of respect in underprivileged communities.

In the late 1980s and early 1990s most of the serious guys

in our communities or hotspots, like Brixton, were from Jamaica. They came over, had their run-ins with the local guys and eventually got their foot in the door because of their violent nature, resilience and determination - sometimes just because of their mouth. Everything about them was different and they brought about 70% of the gun violence in black communities in England. So this was the environment that I was in and, needless to say, as time went on I myself ended up in conflict with some of them. Every time this happened I would shut them down, and by this stage the community was with me because I was not pointing my gun at them, the poor weak and helpless. I would only confront strong people who were in the same game, and also I would always be happy to give money to people, especially women or children.

Alliances and friendships in those times were stronger and more intimate than today and there were only a small number of people who were about the same thing. Therefore, if you were a gunman, you would know nearly every other gunman within the black community in London. That way, problems could be resolved more easily and people who were not really like that would not give you any resistance, because it was an unknown and new phenomenon. Meanwhile, the police were basically playing catch-up - not really caring, because the victims were black.

Some time along the way of my burglary escapades, I ended up getting nicked for burglary and possession of an offensive weapon, and was eventually sentenced to three years' imprisonment. On the day of my sentence, I realised while on the bus being taken back to Brixton prison that my handcuffs were loose so I slipped them off my wrist. When we got to Brixton High Road I made one almighty jump for the door, because at the time there was a prison officers' strike on and they were taking us in coaches. Needless to say, as the door opened, one of them managed to grab the back of my jumper and pulled me back onto the bus. The bus went straight to Brixton prison, not stopping for traffic lights or anything, and once inside the prison, I got an almighty beating for my troubles.

While I was away serving my three years, Steve went on to develop a full formula of burglary mixed with robbery. They would go all around the M25 and pick out Lloyds banks where old-fashioned buildings still remained. Then, they would simply cut the bars the night before, so that at 5 o'clock or 5.30, when the bank closed, mind you, this being winter so it's dark, they would just pop in and rob the bank. They netted around a million pounds, but as with everything else that doesn't go along the grain, or general cycle of life in society, you have to be lucky every single day. The police only have to be lucky once, and they did get lucky once, and Steve got 12 years for his troubles.

I did my three years, came out and decided that I was going to be more direct about how I got my own money and what I did next. That was the point when the gun really came into my life full-time. Everything from then on started to revolve around robberies of some form or another. On one occasion I got £70,000 to share between four people, and with my cut of that money I went to Jamaica for the first time as an adult.

Chapter 5
Escape from prison

Any time I was in prison, escape was always in the back of my mind, and with the mindset I had at the time I just believed in myself that I could do anything I put my mind to. In the end, the way it actually happened was what some people would call a fluke. Others would say it was God's will.

It definitely did happen though. It all started with me getting arrested for the armed robbery of a post office in Leicestershire. Allegedly, the car of which the number plate was taken down by a member of the public had half a fingerprint inside the glass of the front passenger seat. Therefore, that is evidence and you are nicked - simple as that.

It was alleged that four individuals broke into a house that was connected to a post office, in an all-in one style building. I was one of the suspects. Of the other three people in question, one of them used to live in Balham, and we all used to drop round there a lot, as his house was like a social hub for us as friends. It was a big Victorian house, with a communal door and then two separate front doors inside, and you could see the street from inside the living room.

On this particular day, I went around to my friend's house, but as soon as I got there I didn't feel right, and something made me look out of the window. The moment I did, everything just got hyper-fast, because there were two massive SPG vans outside. The police in riot gear came flying out of the van, taking off the door - all in a matter of seconds. I managed to jump out of the back window and landed in the back garden, and to tell the truth if I had turned to the right and put all of my heart into it, I believe to this day I might have had a slim chance of getting away, but I could hear radios in the bushes, which automatically told me that the back was covered too. It was dark, and by this time I was known as a gunman, and guns were used in the alleged offence, for which they were kicking off the door, so in my own calculations I came to the conclusion that in microseconds they would be right there, and that they would no doubt find a very good explanation or reason for shooting me. For that reason, I hid in some bushes in the corner of garden as it was quite large. However, needless to say, I got arrested, as did my friend and his female partner. It was like that house was just having a bad luck day.

But my other friend, the final suspect in this scenario, had quite different luck. He was in a minicab on his way to the same flat and he saw all the commotion and just told the driver to keep driving. He was like: 'Driver, don't stop at all.' Laugh out loud.

So me and my co-d got arrested for armed robbery and false imprisonment, and then after a few weeks of being on remand, they found some fibres on my third co-defendant and he ended up with us. So there we were, three of us now in total, on remand for these very serious charges. That last co-d was the youngest of us all, and to be frank, at the time, the stupidest but, as luck would have it, the fibres on his clothes were the only evidence against him so eventually he was released halfway through the trial.

My situation was totally different; I knew that I was looking at a long sentence and the chances of getting a not guilty were slim. We ended up having a lot of internal politics between us, over how we should all move forward, and, for some reason, that same young guy went and told his solicitor that me and my other co-defendant were putting pressure on him to plead guilty. Also, prior to that, the prison had had enough of me in general anyway, because of my general attitude and my ability to pull people together.

There were two local guys in that prison who the officers

were definitely afraid of. Looking back, I believe that with one of them this was because he seemed to know where a lot of the officers lived, or he could find out, and the other one was a handful, full stop. They are both dead now, and both died the way they lived - violently. The first one's name was Eugene. He was a small guy, but had a lot of front and it was a powerful combination in that little pond because we were in Leicester prison at the time, which is a small local prison, old Victorian style with extremely high walls around it. Eugene was born and bred in Leicester and therefore seemed to know everybody. The second man I knew as Tucker,

Around the same time as my co-d's solicitor sending the letter, complaining about his client being under pressure, the kitchen, whether deliberately or accidentally, gradually downgraded the quality of the food to a terrible standard. That prison is not one where you can cook your own food, like you can in the high security estate, ie in the prisons that housed Category A prisoners, so everyone relied on the prison food.

On this particular day, they served us some stone cold food and nobody was happy. So I just seized the moment for confrontation, because I knew that everybody was in agreement. As soon as I started talking out loud about the quality of the food, Eugene jumped in and punched an officer in his face and then started running up and down the landing, screaming and ranting. Everybody else was just bunching up into corners, causing the staff to be even more spooked.

I have never seen hot food appear so fast in all of my life - cheeseburger and chips for everybody. But at the same time, as you might notice, the general theme is that in this system, no matter what happens, some prisoner will get the blame, and nobody will accept that the food was terrible and cold and they were in the wrong. So they put me straight in the segregation unit. Then, a few hours later, I saw my door open and there were about 30 prisoners and two prison officers standing there, with Eugene at the front, saying that they wanted to make sure that I was okay. Then he passed me a pen and paper and gave me a look towards the pen, letting me know that there was something inside it. It turned out to be a small piece of cannabis, but under the circumstances it was more than appreciated and I went to my bed feeling like a man.

Needless to say, after the letter that was it. The governor came to me and said: 'Right, where do you wish to go, because we cannot keep you here any longer?' So I said 'Anywhere down south', and I ended up in a prison called

Bullingdon, which is in Bicester, Oxfordshire. Compared to Leicester it was nice, because it was brand new and clean inside, and at first the staff were okay. Plus, you had remand prisoners and convicted together, so it made it an environment where there were a lot of things happening and you could get your hands on whatever, from drugs to McDonalds on a visit. It was also the first place in prison that I ever had sex. The first time was a sneaky one by just simply going into the visitors' toilet instead of the prisoners' one, because they were right next door to each other. And then the next time was me just spinning a story about how I was depressed and needed some time to be with my girlfriend, so no one would see me cry, and they put me in a legal visit room and just left us there for an hour.

The visits were very lax also. They would put a blue tag around your bag of clothes that you were allowed in if you were on remand, and once this tag was on the bag it was assumed it had been searched by officers and would just be given to the prisoner. Needless to say, a prisoner got hold of some of the tags. Therefore, some of us had an opportunity to get items into the prison and by fluke I ended up with a flick knife. At this stage there was not a direct plan for the knife, apart from that it seemed a thing worth having.

Then one day, I asked an officer for a phone call, because

I had run out of phone cards. This officer was young and cheeky and he told me no. And when he said no, he did not do it in a nice way. The structure of each wing inside this prison is one where there are landings above landings. Therefore, if you go upstairs and throw something downstairs and then just move back against the wall, no-one downstairs would know who did what. And that is exactly what happened, because somebody threw hot water down onto that same officer that told me no, and when they threw it down on him, they did not do it in a nice way either. So we had him screaming, the alarm bell going off and some prisoners backing up and others laughing. Me? I was in my cell.

Once there's an incident inside prison, they automatically lock up everybody. That's the first thing they do, so that is what happened next. I had a cellmate and I don't know what possessed him to do this, but about one hour after the incident, when by now there were about 30 officers standing around on the landings, deciding whose head they were going to kick in, my cellmate pressed the cell bell and told officers that he was the one who assaulted the officer with the hot water.

Needless to say, they took him to segregation. In the back of my mind I was still saying to myself that that was not going to pacify them and that they knew the truth. Just as I thought, a few hours later they came for me and put me in the segregation unit too. Me and the staff in the seg unit then spent the next day mouthing off at each other. I was telling them they'd better hope I don't get a not guilty. So they decided that they would get two local prisoners and spin them a story that I was a sex offender, in order to get me assaulted properly in a way that they knew they could not get away with themselves. So, lo and behold, next day comes and the officers are like: 'You can go on the wing now Smith, but it's a new wing and we have heard rumours that you won't be safe up there'.

I started laughing at this and told them to hurry up and bring me onto whatever wing they were bringing me to. So they put me on this new wing. It was first thing in the morning and I can remember going to the servery to get some milk, so I could make some breakfast, and these two big white guys behind the hotplate were giving me dirty looks and I just felt the vibes that I should watch them. About two minutes later, my cell door opens and another white guy that knew me from the other wing and also knew my charges, which were armed robbery and firearms, told me that the staff were trying to get me assaulted, by telling those two lads that I was a sex offender, but he put them straight. Then the two lads came over to me and shook my hand, so that was it.

The staff are fuming now, because nothing they tried worked and they just decided they was gonna ship me back to where I'd come from. As luck would have it, they just grabbed up all of my stuff, stuffed it into bags and sealed it, and the knife was in one of the bags. I got back to Leicester prison and the governor came and said to me in the reception area: 'Smith you will have to go to segregation for tonight and tomorrow we're going to send you to Brixton prison and that will be your last chance to stay on the landing and behave until your trial. Otherwise we're going to keep you in the segregation unit until your trial, no matter how many months it takes to come.'

So I was like 'okay, governor' and I just went with the staff to the segregation unit. Ten minutes later an officer just opened my door and brought in the bags from the other prison with the tags on, without searching them, and bang that was it. I had a knife and I knew that I was travelling to Brixton, south London, my own area. I just had to try something. I just felt like it was my duty to escape, so the next morning I got up really early and wrapped some plastic around a little square of soap and then tied a piece of string onto it. Then I tied that to the knife and put it up – I'm sure you can guess where! - because I knew that the first and hardest hurdle to get past was being searched. Then, I went through all the searching procedure and it worked! Then after being searched, I was in the room waiting to go and I just pulled the string which had the piece of soap on the other end, and now I had the knife!

I unlocked it and put in my waistband, so I knew that once the handcuffs were on I could still use my other hand to get it. We started to walk towards the last gate before getting into the vehicle and one of the officers turns round to me and says 'I know you Smith, you sure you haven't got anything on you?' and then he started giving me another pat down. I thought quick and just started laughing and saying to him, 'Are you mad? Didn't you just search me?' and then he just stopped. That was how close it came to not ever happening.

So we get into the car with two officers and a driver, so that's three. And as we start driving down the motorway towards London, one of the officers was boasting to his friend that he had upset some big Mafia boss, Francesco Di Carlo, who was at the time in the special unit in Leicester prison, and he seemed very pleased that he was in a position to be able to do this. Meanwhile I'm sitting in between the two of them with a newspaper on my lap with my left hand underneath it with the knife. At the time it was very exciting and I could feel the adrenaline building up and then the driver of the car started saying things like 'It's really bad around here', when we got into South London.

Then we get to Clapham South next to the South Circular and this man is not sure of the way and, get this, is willing to let me, the prisoner, give him directions. I kid you not. This is how it went. So I was more than happy to give him directions and directed him onto one of the side streets of the South Circular Road. I remember saying to him, 'Take a right, then a left.' And he said to me 'What was that? Left?' and I said 'Yes', and then as he took the left it started. I just grabbed the one I was handcuffed to, put the knife to his throat and started screaming at the top of my voice to undo the fucking handcuffs or I was going to cut his throat. The other officer with the key was like 'All right Smith, all right Smith' and he undid the handcuffs

Then I told the driver to leave the fucking keys in the car ignition and get the fuck out of the car now, and he did not need to be told twice. So now I've got total control of the situation and had turned the tables on them. My God did it feel nice. I held onto the one that I had the knife to, and came out of the car and then pushed him onto the other two officers. Then I jumped into the driver's seat of the car, which happened to be a BMW five series, put it into first gear and revved it up, and then put it into second and redlined it.

I was alive. I'd done it. One minute I was in captivity and looking at 12 years and the next minute I was free, or should I say 'at large' – it still amounts to the same thing. I only had to drive a few roads to find shelter and then I went to friends and on the way out I saw another friend who took me to a house and told me I could stay there for the day until night-time. I then used that time, which was about five hours, to get people to bring me my gun, money and a car. I left my friend's house with my pistol and a sawn-off shotgun. It was on.

I left London that night and spent a few days in Bristol in order to acquire a false passport in a friend's name, which I collected from the passport office in Wales. In all, it was just five days from my escape before I was on a plane to Jamaica, carrying my new false passport and about £10,000 in cash.

Chapter 6

Jamaica

Jamaica was really electrifying for me every day. The underprivileged side of Jamaica was conducive with my own lifestyle. Then it soon also became apparent that it was a part of the world where cocaine costs a fraction of the price in England, so I was like 'happy days'. Jamaica is not an island that has social security; there is nobody there to give any handouts of any form, so basically you have to feed those below and survive on your own and do whatever it takes. That in itself makes it a place where very few questions are asked and people are more than willing to do things they most probably would not if their life was not so desperate. In any case, I started to have a nice time going to parties at night and to the beach in the daytime and I was getting money sent over regularly by Western Union, meeting lots of girls on the beach and also having girls coming from England to see me.

One of my cousins happened to be friends with that area's leader or don. He is still alive as we speak, but now lives in Canada, I'll call him Cassie. He was basically a bully and controlled the community by fear of the guns. Life was okay for a bit. I had a nice car and the island was very mystical, so you could drive around and see a cow or goat walking down the road like a human being, looking left or right for traffic; or you might see a hummingbird eating from the flowers - something so beautiful on an island full of so much pain and suffering. One of the guys from England was an older guy than me and somebody at the time that I could look up to, as a more serious person than myself. I'll call him Ray. He was a good guide for the most part, and only did big robberies. |In the beginning that was the real reason that I looked up to him, plus, he always tried to be there for me as I was growing up. You also have to remember, that at this time on the streets in England, if you were a knifeman and willing to use it, you would have a certain amount of respect and guns only came into it with a very few black guys, who either knew white guys to buy them from or stumbled across them in various different ways, such as burglaries, and that these guns would be used mainly for money, not in the sense of literally using them, but in order to frighten people into believing that you would use them.

So anyway, I'm in Jamaica and he was also there, but living in a different part of Kingston. Unbeknown to me, he had gotten himself into a verbal altercation with somebody he viewed as a friend at first, a local Jamaican who took the altercation personal and decided it was time to take revenge on my friend. So on the day that I turned up with a lot of suitcases and two foreign girls, this new enemy of my friend was watching everything. I was happy to see my friend and I said to him that we should all go out to a party or dance hall and listen to a sound system.

Stone Love sound system was held at the time every Thursday night at the crossroads between up and downtown Kingston, in a venue that was called House of Leo. Ray declined my offer and the two girls also said they were tired, so I decided to go to the dance with my group of Jamaican friends from my part of Kingston. I had a nice night. Then the next day when I went back to Ray's house, the man had a big bandage around his head and around his arms. At first I assumed he had crashed his motorbike or something. Then I noticed the iron bars that secure the house had been cut and, before I could say anything, he started to explain to me what had happened to him, along with his auntie and the two girls. Basically, that same person that he had had the altercation with had sent for four gunmen from a place called Rima, a very dangerous place in Kingston. They came and cut the telephone wire. (At that time there were not really mobile phones so that made you trapped in the house.) They then used a welding torch to cut the iron bars and enter the house - his auntie's husband hid in a cupboard that was so small it was comical.

Then the robbers proceeded to fire rounds into the ceiling and smashed my friend's head with the butt of the gun, demanding that he tell them where the money was. I give him credit, he did not tell them so they stabbed him in his arm with an ice pick, fired more rounds into the ceiling and then took whatever they could see.

The girls woke up because of all of the noise; they had been asleep in the back house, which was part of the main house, which the gunmen had not noticed for some reason, so they never even saw them. But what they did see was enough for one of the girls to faint on the spot, after seeing all of the blood and bullet holes in the ceiling. So here we go, now we've got a problem, and a big one too, which involves pride, local status and the fact that these guys are thinking that we are soft and weak because we come from England

After seeing all of that madness that had gone on, I went straight back to my own community and related to the main man what had happened. Then I went back to Ray. All of the people who were genuine towards him had gotten together a small arsenal, consisting of an A1 M-16 and a pump-action rifle. Both these items of course are very hard to hide on your person and, if you were travelling through Kingston with them, you would basically have to dress up as police officers and drive with them in the open. I was not keen on this idea, but I did agree that we should get them back, so I took it upon myself to ask someone in my community to get a handgun.

The day came to buy the handgun. Ray came with me, and another Jamaican from my community - a top man, but I naïvely believed he could do what I asked him to do - so there we were, three of us in my car going to a community called Granspen - a very dangerous lawless place, and lo and behold, they wanna do the deal at night. This in itself told us that something was not right and when we got there the man from my community and the go-between from Granspen who was in my car at the time was told by two guys to go with him to collect the handgun. This was a security move to make sure that his man was out of the firing line when it went down like they had already planned, so that left three people in the car – me, Ray and my Jamaican friend. I was just in the middle of saying 'Is this really wise, this deal at night?' when out of nowhere the gunmen appeared. My car had tints so they could not see inside the car, but I clearly saw them and for some unknown reason they took Ray out first, then the other Jamaican.

At this point I was saying to myself, there is no way under the sun I am going with these guys for them to kill us, or should I say kill me, because at that point I was only concerned about my own life. I saw a handgun in the man's hand and I just grabbed it and started the car in one motion. By then two of the gunmen had taken Ray. Then from nowhere the Jamaican yardie just jumped back in the car window and started fighting the last gunman; he managed to pull out his ice pick, an implement that a lot of men carry in Jamaica that is really designed to break ice. He then proceeded to stab the third gunman, while I was driving up the road with the door open. We got to about 40mph when I heard him scream out and drop off the car. I didn't think he was dead. What I knew was he must've been seriously hurt. But to tell the truth I was just relieved that I was not gonna die on that day.

So then we had to go back to my community and get the don himself to intervene. He was like 'Rudy – you know you could ah drop out just like that?' I was like 'Yeah'. We then jumped into my car with some more man and raced back down to that community, where the attempted robbery had occurred, and saw the don for that community. He said that my friend had been robbed and released and that they only fired a couple of shots over his head, but if they had known that their boy had been stabbed, they would have killed my friend. After that, all I could do was go to Ray's community to see if he made it back. He did and he told me how. He said that after they robbed him of the money he had and the bracelet on his wrist, they said 'Run pussy ', and then fired rounds over his head. He stopped a big man in a car, told him what had happened and begged him for a bus fare and that's how he got home.

So, basically now two big things had happened in a small amount of time and I could see the effect it had on him. To add into the mix, he started a relationship with the girl that I was dealing with not even two months before. So here we are in his community and he's giving me all these sideways looks like he wants harm to come to me. I read the play and just said to him 'Everybody's got their own road to go down', and basically that was the last I ever saw of him.

My life just carried on, all parties. More girls flying in and out, with everybody saying yes to anything I said

Chapter 7

Attempted murder and on the run

I eventually left Jamaica, on the back of people in my own community pointing the finger at me over a murder, which I did not do. Jamaica is Jamaica though and once this starts to happen, it is wise to take yourself away from all of it, because it will not end up well. So there I was, on an aeroplane, on a false passport, because by this time I was already wanted by every police agency.

My flight stopped at Miami and I made a phone call to England, only to be told that there was some kind of robbery that had gone on and I was £20,000 out of pocket. So by the time I was on my next flight from Miami to London, I was not in a good mood. I landed at Heathrow Airport and phoned the person responsible, because I actually knew him and his family very well.

The individual decided that he wasn't gonna respond to my way of resolving everything, ie give back what you took and I don't shoot you. Instead the guy wanted to play tough and put his family in danger and this resulted in me ending up shooting up his mom's house. From that moment on, things just started to get very fast. People just dialling in people to get robbed and I was obliging, so over a seven-week period a lot of things happened. Every other day there was action and I would have a semi-automatic pistol with me at all times, and I would sleep in different places every night with it under my pillow. In fact, it never used to be more than an arm's length away from me at any time. At this stage I was of the view that I would sooner send anybody to hospital, in order not to end up in there myself. The gun was a Sig Sauer p226 – it was such good a weapon that the British police still use it today.

In between all of this, I got the drop on a jeweller's in south west London and I thought this would also be a straightforward scenario, but the guys it belonged to had a lot of heart and put up one almighty fight. In the melee I could see the piles of £50 notes, but too much was happening to even pick them up and I did not want to leave nobody behind, so it ended up me having to let a few rounds go in the ceiling just for us to get out of there. We did get out, but I left some little drips of blood at the scene, so in the end I got caught and eventually got 14 years for my troubles. The people who owned the shop were not so gangster that they were about to leave it at that, and they were more than happy to come to court. So there you go -

you got your Justice.

But for now I was still free, and not long after this, that fateful life-changing night came. It came by default because I did not wake up planning to do anything to any police, but I had allowed myself to be surrounded by people who did not have the same heart as me, and who were just there for the ride, the money and an easy life. One of them I will just call Red Boy. Obviously this is a red-skinned guy, and at the time he was a friend, or a yes-man friend, but his problem was he didn't know how to follow orders and did not do things the way you told him to. Not understanding that I had more insight into what I was trying to achieve and he did not need to worry about it; he just needed to understand how to do what I was telling him. On this day, someone owed me a few thousand pounds, but it was a friend (Bruckfoot Patrick RIP) and I never had any problems with him about money. So I told Red Boy to collect it, but he went and did not collect the money. Not the end of the world though, so I asked the person that I was with that day, who had a motorbike, if he could give me a lift to the pub in Brixton to collect the money that Red Boy had not collected. Can you see now how small things started to unravel into big things, because now I have to collect the money myself?

This part of my book and life story was always going to be hard to write because I am mindful that this is not the 1990s and it is now 2016 and the Metropolitan Police have got the biggest body of professional gunmen, who might read the book and take it personally, or the wrong way, when in fact all I am doing is putting my life story out there, in the hope that it prevents anybody else, especially underprivileged young black men from taking the same path. Because I am an observer of mankind, I am able to translate my life story into a book form, so I can die as an author and not as a gunman, or criminal, with no other redeeming features. Therefore, I would appreciate if the powers-that-be take this book as a positive and not a negative. If this country where I was born is so open and embracing and fair, then I deserve another chance just like anybody else. So time will tell.

Continuing where I left off the story with Red Boy, we get to Brixton. I am a bit cautious on a bike if somebody else is riding it because I have a problem with trusting their ability to keep us safe and alive on the bike, but one thing I can say for sure about my rat co-defendant is he could ride a motorbike very, very well.

So we get to Coldharbour Lane, where the pub was situated

that my friend Patrick was in. On the way into the pub, I noted a police Sierra, which was an old-fashioned police car of the time, observing us as we went to the pub. I was not unduly concerned and just went into the pub, where I saw my friend, resolved the situation about the money and went to leave. This is where it all starts.

My co-defendant's motorbike had a delayed reaction alarm on it. That means that, if you touched it prematurely, it would cut out and you would have to wait for one minute to start the engine again. So as we came out of the pub and went to the bike, my co-defendant sees a white guy that he knew and started talking to him, and while doing so he accidentally touched the bike, which kicked in the cut-out system for one minute. Right on cue, as the white guy walked off, the police Sierra car came round the corner and stopped right in front of us. In the back of my mind, I was like 'Here we go'.

Now we must remember that at this stage I'm already wanted for escaping from prison, armed robbery and firearms offences. I've got a 9mm Sig Sauer pistol in my waistband and the spare magazine in my pocket, plus drugs, so I know that if I let the officers put handcuffs on me, they are not coming back off for at least a decade. In my mind everything is happening in microseconds, and the fear of going to prison just outweighed everything else.

So they stopped, got out of the car and started with my co-defendant due to the fact that it was his bike, and this man, my co-defendant, starts saying things like 'I haven't got nothing to hide, I haven't got nothing to hide', and I am thinking to myself 'Is this guy trying to set me up or something? Why is he saying these things?'

So then they turned their attention to me because they noticed that I was moving away from them, trying to make space between us. Then one of them said something along the lines of 'Stay there a minute fella, stay there a minute fella', and that was it.

It just all kicked in; there is no other way to explain it. When you're a person that has experience of guns you understand the mindset behind it and the tactical way in which to get the most out of the actual weapon. So from the point where I decide I am not willing to get arrested - and the fear of prison overrides the fear of anything else - I now know that I have to, for want of a better expression, put these two men in a position where they cannot do anything for a few minutes.

In hindsight, this could have been done a lot of different ways, but all of the other ways would take more time. For example, I could have tried to tell them to lie on the floor or I could have just shot the car tyres out, so they couldn't chase us. But a lot of factors came into play and the English police, by their very nature, are not into complying with anything or anyone, to an extent that is unbelievable, because in lots of other countries if you're a police officer and you get caught on the wrong end of a gun you comply.

So I know none of this is gonna happen and I've got at most 90 seconds before my window of opportunity leaves me. The adrenaline kicked in and I remember drawing the gun and shooting the first one in the leg. That in itself shows that I did not sign up to be no cop killer. He went down and his friend spun around and tried to run off. My co-defendant dropped his gloves and also tried to run off. I spontaneously fired one round at the officer that was running and it hit him in his back; then the other round went into the air to control my co-defendant before he could run away and leave me with a bike I don't know how to ride. That soon stopped him in his tracks and I was like: 'The bike, get on the fucking bike!'

So we jumped on the bike and blew off up the lane at up to 100mph, and all along my co-defendant just kept saying my nickname over and over again: 'Skeema man, Skeema man' like a scratched record. I banged him in the side of his ribs with the butt of the gun, just to remind him who had the power.

We got to Brixton Hill roundabout and he seemed as if he wanted to stop at the lights, but I brandished the gun at the line of cars and every single one of them stopped. We flew up Tulse Hill to Norwood, where I promptly jumped off the motorbike, discarded my crash helmet and jacket under a car, and jumped into a mini-cab.

The cab drove me to the safe house, where I changed my clothes and my gun, to avoid ballistic evidence, grabbed my false passport and £5,000, and then went to another safe house, where I started making frantic phone calls everywhere until I got a driver to come and pick me up. He took me to Harwich or some ferry port in the middle of nowhere; I stayed in a hotel for the night, bought a rucksack in the morning and jumped on the ferry to Holland. Within 48 hours, I was in another country continuing with my life in the same vein that I had been living it in England. For me at the time it was just another incident and another

the depth to which the Triad societies had infiltrated the Chinese community in Glasgow and the power they wield through extortion, drugs and gambling." The police were unable to charge anyone with the murder largely because witnesses were too frightened to testify. Triads use intimidation, and the inbred fear of their organisation to prevent members of the Chinese community from informing against them.

The influence and power of the Yardies has gradually grown along with the boom in crack cocaine. Although predictions that Britain was going to face an American-style "invasion" by West Indian gangsters has proved unfounded, in recent years the police have reported an upsurge in violent Yardie drug wars.

John Brennan, detective sergeant of the South-East Regional Crime Squad and one of the country's leading experts on Yardies, says that the Jamaican gangs now control most of the supply of crack cocaine in London, Manchester, Birmingham, Nottingham, Leeds and Bristol.

Yardies often use brutal tactics against rivals. In 1991 in north London a Nigerian drugs courier had her face and breasts ironed by a drugs gang to obtain details of her shipment. Boiling water was poured over her head when she passed out during the torture.

In March 1994 a cocaine dealer shot two unarmed policemen – in the back and in the leg – as they carried out a routine check in a south London street. Leroy Smith, who was convicted in February of attempted murder, had boasted to his girlfriend: "Those two deserved to get it. I should have got them good and proper."

Japanese Yakuza gangs and the Italian Mafia have also established themselves in Britain, primarily via money-laundering. But the most recent threat to Britain, according to both police and NCIS, are criminals from the former Soviet Union. The break-up of the USSR, they argue, has resulted in weakened or non-existent border checks and a gradual decline in law and order. This has enabled gangs to exploit weak banking regulations in their own countries to launder money through the UK. There have also been fears that increasing numbers of firearms will be smuggled into the country.

Organised crime is alive and kicking in Britain. But despite the glum predictions, British police have as yet found no evidence to suggest that Britain is likely to be overwhelmed by gangs or run by a "godfather" figure. As the Home Affairs Select Committee concluded: "Organised crime raises images of the Mafia or the Krays ... but to confine concern to such relatively tightly organised groups would be to miss most of today's criminal activity which, if more loosely organised, is nevertheless actually more threatening."

25 years for drug dealer who shot police

BY JASON BENNETTO
Crime Correspondent

A drug dealer made a mock gun with his hands and pretended to fire at two police officers whom he had previously shot as he was led to his cell after being jailed for 25 years yesterday.

Leroy Smith, 26, remained remorseless throughout his trial at the Old Bailey. The jury heard how he had gone on a year-long shooting rampage after escaping from three prison officers by holding one at knife-point.

Judge Richard Lowry told him: "Dreadful crimes must attract dreadful sentences."

Smith, of Wandsworth, south London, shot Constable James Seymour, 31, in the back and his colleague, Constable Simon Carroll, 23, in the leg when they approached him outside a pub in Brixton, south London, in March last year.

He later told his girlfriend: "The buzzards deserved it," and added. "I should've got them good and proper."

She also said that Smith was besotted with his 9mm firearm with an infra-red ray to guide the bullets. He had boasted that police would never catch him, because if anyone got in his way he would shoot them.

After firing at the officers, Smith escaped on a motorbike and fled to America – where he was arrested in connection with another shooting last July.

Smith, who had links with Yardie drug gangs, organised couriers to bring crack cocaine into this country, the court was told. He was also accused of using his gun to frighten off rival drug dealers.

He was on the run when the officers were shot. He had escaped in April 1993 while being transferred from Leicester to Brixton prison after his arrest on gun charges.

Smith was jailed for two years for that escape, 18 years for a firearms offence, and five years for robbery. He was given a 25-year sentence for attempting to murder PC Seymour and 18 years for wounding PC Carroll. The judge ordered all the sentences to run concurrently. Smith denied all the charges.

newspaper clipping; none of the magnitude of the things I was doing really hit home. Maybe that was because I was still at large.

Holland

I remember being on the ferry, as England got smaller and smaller, and it just felt right. My troubles were getting further and further away. That was an overwhelming feeling.

It also struck me how huge the actual ferry was, as it was the first time I'd been on one. Once I arrived in Holland I jumped into a minicab, to take me from the ferry port to Amsterdam. The first thing I noticed was how new all of the minicabs were i.e. brand-new Mercedes.

I arrived at Amsterdam, booked into a hotel and put all my jewellery and money in the hotel's safe. Bear in mind that I am now in a foreign country and unarmed. So my normal habit of going around with a 36-ounce gold chain around my neck, a £8,000 Zenith wrist watch and a few carat diamond ring was not a good advertisement, considering I was not and am not a very physical person. Most of my power is psychological and I understood as a robber that anybody could get robbed, hence leaving all the obvious items of high value in the safe.

I then cashed some sterling for a few hundred Dutch guilders and hit the streets. The first thing that came to mind was that this was like a big Oxford Street, with what seemed like millions of people around, and then there was loads of African guys on the sidewalks selling heroin and coke. That was also the first time I'd ever seen a girl half naked in a shop window for sale. Even by my standards, that was on a different level.

As a whole, Dutch people seemed soft, but looking back now, I would say they were civil and probably educated, and that's why they appeared that way at the time, considering the monster I had become.

I stayed in Holland for a few days, and then took an aeroplane to JF Kennedy airport, New York, on my false passport. When I landed I made the mistake of rushing to get my luggage and this made the custom officers pull me over. They then took me into a side room. Bearing in mind that only days before the incident had happened with the police, so I did not need this, but I also knew that they would be working off of my false identity, and that I had come from Holland and not England, so the chances of them knowing who I really was were remote, but nevertheless it was a situation.

They searched me and started saying things like: 'Things just don't sound right here, man, Level with us.' And I just kept saying the same thing. I have come to America for a short holiday to see my family.' And then one of the officers found a piece of paper on me, which was essentially a prayer which one can do when travelling and he just seemed to calm down. Then he whispered something to his friend and they let me go. That was it. I just hightailed it out of there and jumped into a minicab to South Bronx, where I was told by the minicab driver: 'This is a very dangerous place.' LOL.

Chapter 8

USA

My first opinion of America was like 'Wow gunman's paradise' because it seemed as if it was a free for all and every other person had access. Therefore, if you got into a confrontation it could lead into a shoot-out very fast indeed, and everybody seemed at least to be up for it.

I got a new car and I contacted my friends in Jamaica, who promptly put me in touch with people who had the same outlook in life at that time as me; in other words, they were quite happy to sell drugs and shoot people.

I also had a problem of securing something for my personal protection, so my cousin got me a link to buy a 38 Smith & Wesson long barrel. These only have six shots to their name, but they could get you out of trouble. At the time that was the service revolver for a lot of police in New York, until they got Glocks as side-arms.

Needless to say, it didn't take long for one of my Jamaican friends in America to make contact. He was based in Connecticut and had been there for a long time, maybe eight years or so, and in that time, he and his friends had been in a year-long war with another set of Jamaicans called the Rats. On the first day we met, he took me to a corner which belonged to them and introduced me to the rest of his people. This one guy Pepper was in a wheelchair, permanently paralysed from being in a shoot-out. But even as a man in a wheelchair, he had still got a gun on him.

There was a red X marked on the floor outside the shop on the corner where I was standing and I asked about it and was told that another person just like me, had come to hang around them for a while and the other side, ie the Rats, saw him in my new social circle and shot him on the spot. So the X was in remembrance of that guy. The atmosphere was one of mistrust in every direction, so, even if somebody was to come up to the corner to buy a bag of weed, everybody was twitching and getting into position, in case it turned out to be gun play. Most people were standing next to a car or a bollard, anything that's tough enough to deflect the bullets when they were whizzing around. The same Jamaican – I'll just call him Mike - was well connected in Connecticut so it didn't take long before he had introduced me to an estate agent who did everything in cash, and I ended up with a condominium. Then girls started coming over to spend time with me, and we used to party every night and go to nightclubs, eight cars deep. And over there at that time police officers would be on the doors of the nightclubs, so everybody left their guns in the car

On the way home when everyone's stoned and tipsy, people would be like 'What you got?' One man will be like 'a Glock'. Another man would be like: 'I've got a Mac 11'. At the time I had never fired that weapon. I was like: 'Let me test it', and the guy gave it to me. We were driving down the freeway, so it is basically an empty road. The big road signs every few miles can be used as a target, so I wound down the window and touched the trigger once for about two seconds and half of the 32-clip was gone. Man's in the car laughing and saying 'That's about half of a clip, Rudy'.

Then someone else would say to someone else: 'What you got?' He said 'A Beretta', and then the same thing happened again. That guy gave it a go because he'd never tried it before. That was my life - fast and very reckless - a road that I would not advise anybody to go down, because it is very addictive and it always ends badly. It is all a matter of time - you might get five years as a run, but after that, unless you're working with something you're not meant to be working with, the odds will be stacking up against you. It hurts me to see that, after 20 years, a large majority of young black guys still think this road is paved with gold. Let me tell you brother, from the heart, you're only fooling yourself. These are not the words of a broken man; these are words of a wise man and, just like me, you can find something that you can do to enhance your life in a positive way, that makes your family proud, rather than leaving them in tears.

At one stage, I had four girls living in my condominium and I was sleeping with all of them. The sexiest one was called Aisha, so she had my bed; we shared it and others would all be trying to take her place. There were days and times when I would just pick one of them because they were all vying for my attention. On one occasion, which I remember like it was yesterday, I was in bed with Aisha and felt like having a soft drink, so I went downstairs to the kitchen and one of the girls was on the settee watching telly naked, nothing on apart from her knickers. I remember just leaning over, pulling her knickers to the side and slipping it in, and she in turn started to push it back on me, and it turned into some explosive sex. Then I went back upstairs to my bed with Aisha. It was a very empowering feeling.

There was one African girl in the bunch, who I also knew from England. She was a friend of my girlfriend at the time and she was a heavy coke user. A lot of people used to smoke coke in spliffs and it was normal to a certain extent or much more socially acceptable than today. It so happened that a few of my Jamaican friends had already slept with her and I am funny about who I sleep with and who has slept with them, so for me that was out of the question where me and her was concerned. I believe this made negative vibes between us. Anyway, she asked to come to America and money is money, so I told her she could come and she stayed with me for a while, then went to Jamaica and came back to America.

At the time all of my friends were full-blown gunmen and killers, and none of them smoked A class drugs or agreed with it being smoked, or trusted anybody who smoked it. Therefore, if somebody is living in your house and smoking it and someone else comes and smells it, this would put me in a very dangerous position, because there's nothing stopping them from deciding that I am worth the risk for maybe 100 grand, and as I'm already wanted for police shootings, they could just as easily decide to kill me and put me in a dumpster and take what I've got. These were the characters that I was associated with, so there was no way on earth I was gonna let this little crackhead girl jeopardise my life, because, if truth be told, I used to smoke a spliff occasionally laced with coke, and did not want to be in a position to have to explain anything about anything to do with such things, so I told her on the first occasion not to do it and locked everything away.

At the same time this was going on, she kept on goading me, asking me silly questions about my friend in Jamaica, who was the don for that corner, and I took great offence to this, because no one was scared of anyone else in that circle, because we were all armed and had seen action; that was the reality of the circle. The fact that she knew he could get people shot with just a word must have got to her head, so I put her straight and then, lo and behold, the next day I went out when I came back home the house stunk of cocaine again. This was the last straw so I phoned her so-called ex-partner, my friend the don in Jamaica, and told him what she had done.

Later on, when I was arrested, she alleged that I shot at her with a Mac-11 and that she escaped, running into a hospital, screaming, and called the FBI to tell them about my condominium, where I was arrested with a Mac-11 on me. The condo was also searched and found to be in a factory situation, due to a large amount of cocaine and cannabis being found on the premises. They also found a Glock-21 in the kitchen.

The irony of all of this was that, a week prior, one of my friends saw me eating cornflakes and he said to me: 'You are eating prison food'. Then, the same day, we were driving and parked up somewhere, and one of the guys said 'Damn - 18 months in that motherfucker, man!', and when he said that I turned around and looked and saw the prison, and lo and behold, that was the very same prison that I ended up in after this girl sent FBI to my house. The police put her under protection, so she had the nerve to come to England and come to court and tell lies, in return for a free flat and other inducements. Then she wrote some tacky articles in cheap magazines that pay £200 or so for the stories. Hope it was worth it. The mind is a blank canvas, or at least it starts as a blank canvas. Then all of the actions, deeds and things that you do and see, the brain, soaks them up, and in the long run there is a consequence for every action; even if it's not physical, it could be psychological.

So here I was in Bridport Correctional Centre. Everything inside that place is electronically controlled, with one or two guards in a circle surrounded by glass. When it was food time, the doors would open electronically, and you would walk out into the area where the trays would be given out through a slit inside the glass, and then the trays would have to be passed around clockwise until everybody ended up with one plate of food. You couldn't just take a plate of food without passing the tray around and then just start eating it or you couldn't lean over somebody's food; anything at all could lead to confrontation because this was an extremely confrontational place. The truth is that Americans can naturally fistfight; it is normal to them, so most things get resolved in that way, or worse.

Once the article inside the Bridport Post came out it was spread around about me and that was it. They put me in a secure unit without access to anybody, and this disgusting correctional officer by the name of Summers kept coming to my door asking me: 'What happened on the back of the bike? What happened on the back of the bike?' I said to him: 'I don't know what you're talking about'. There were two other guys who were also in the unit with me and we could talk through the glass and they said 'Watch that fat cunt', and they were right, because he ended up giving evidence at my trial.

I was returned to England on board an aeroplane, with five agents, handcuffed and with a blanket over me. When we landed, I saw the armed police come on to the aeroplane and read out all of my charges. As soon as we touched the tarmac, they marched me straight off into a double Category A prison van with a fleet of Range Rovers and bikes, and we did not stop at any traffic lights or anything until we got to the police station

Chapter 9

Belmarsh on remand

Belmarsh is one of seven prisons in England which are classed as Category A prisons. These prisons house the most dangerous inmates in the country. Their definition of dangerousness is based on one's individual capability, plus you can be classed as 'high', or even 'exceptional high', risk Category A, according to your access to money and connections. Sometimes police use it as an extra leverage to have their own way with somebody or to make it harder for them, out of spite, by putting them on Category A because they know that this in itself is a hurdle to climb.

The high security estate is used to hold prisoners who are deemed by the state to be dangerous, whether individually, or by their association or connection with criminal or terrorist organisations, with access to large amounts of money and firearms. These are some of the criteria that mean you could end up in one of these establishments, in what is sometimes referred to as the dispersal system. The names of these prisons are Whitemoor, Belmarsh, Wakefield, Woodhill, Long Lartin, Full Sutton and Frankland. Two of them also house remand prisoners, Belmarsh and Woodhill, and the rest are solely for prisoners serving an extremely long time, some of whom never even dream of seeing the day when they might be free again.

When I first arrived at Belmarsh from Camberwell Magistrates' Court, I was taken inside the prison, but we did not stop; we continued driving to what seemed like another prison inside the prison. This smaller prison had its own walls around it, as well as electric gates and cameras everywhere. Then the reception process began. After being searched completely naked, I was taken onto one of the wings. At the time there were four wings, each housing 12 people at the maximum. Inside the wing on the landing were cameras; everywhere apart from inside your cell and inside the shower room was completely covered by CCTV.

It just so happened that when I came onto the landing, it was exercise and I was asked if I wished to join the lads on the yard. I said yes and went out on to the exercise yard. There were about 10 white men of different ages, from say 30 to 60. The lads were very welcoming. One said 'Hi, my name is John'. Another said he was Lenny. Another said Ronnie. Another said Kevin and then someone pointed at one guy and said 'This is Fred West'. I said 'Fred West?' and everybody started laughing. He was in fact, an alleged IRA commander and a very nice man. We had exercise and went back in. I was then told the procedures for making a phone call or getting a visit. You had to submit the names of the people that you wished to talk to or see, and the police would go and see them first to check them out and decide if they wished to give you permission to see such and such a person, unless it was your immediate family. You were really at their mercy as to whether you saw your loved ones again. The visits room was tiny, and an officer sat in on your visit; there was no way you could have a conversation without their hearing every word you said. The place was completely security orientated.

One day on the exercise yard, John turned around and said: 'Do you realise that by the time we are released from this place, we would have eaten an exercise yard full of potatoes?' Everybody started laughing. Then a few weeks later, three bright sparks in the prison's crown at the time, which was HMP Parkhurst, somehow managed to put together a ladder, cloned the key, hid in the gym and made good their escape. If only they had taken the ferry straight away, they would have got to the mainland, but the story goes that they tried to get an aeroplane, but could not find one with a battery and ended up running around the island for days. This caused a lot of blowback from staff and this was the first time that I noticed one of the tactics that they seem to like the most. It was called collective punishment, where everybody suffers for the price of one person so lo and behold, in Belmarsh, hundreds of miles from Parkhurst the staff locked us down and proceeded to rip everything up and take things away. They took a small bottle of perfume from me. It almost brought tears of anger to my eyes that now a little young guy could push me around and I could not do anything about it. Ten months before this I would have shot him for much less.

After this escape, and an earlier one from Whitemoor by IRA prisoners, Michael Howard, who was the Home Secretary at the time, made a set of new rules for prisoners, and created what is now the Incentives and Earned Privileges Scheme, on which prisoners are split into Basic Standard and Enhanced levels. If you are on Basic you get nothing; you are not allowed to wear your own clothes or spend your own money, or to have in-cell TV, which at that time they were planning to introduce in the near future.

While at Belmarsh, I got to understand a lot of things about life in general, politics and people fighting for freedom.

The make-up of the unit that I was on in Belmarsh was two Colombians, three or four armed robbers, (i.e. people who stopped vans or took security vans off the streets and relieved them of their millions), a few English drug dealers and then the last lot were IRA members or alleged IRA members.

On one occasion the wing was locked down because we were having a visit from Michael Howard. Howard went into the cell of one of the Colombians but not into anyone else's. I don't know what was said in there; all I know is that two weeks later a Lear jet came and he was sent back to Colombia, despite him having been charged with 1,000 kg, one metric ton, of cocaine. Draw whatever inference you please! As I said, I started learning how things really went and what really mattered was who you are and who you know, ie connections political or other.

The IRA guys watched their films about 'The Troubles' with pride and felt strong inside themselves in the conviction that they knew why they were there and that there were many more men ready to take their place. They were the backbone of the dispersal system at the time, because for the last 20 years they had fought with the system day and night, sometimes violently, for their rights. Therefore, at that time in 1995, respect for them was high. I remember one day an officer making derogatory remarks about Irish people and one of the IRA lads just walked up to him and punched him in his mouth; then he pointed to the other officers and said 'get him off the wing'. And so it was.

Some time went by and the officers and I was starting to get into it because I was just a young and angry black man who had a lot of issues at the time and I was looking at a life sentence if things did not work out. Most of the time it was verbal, but sometimes also physical, like one day I started on one officer over something he had been meant to do but had not done, and things got heated. Then they said 'It's bang-up time', and everybody started to get locked away in their cells. After bang-up they would bring the food round to your cells, going round from cell one to 12. But then I noticed that, instead of starting with my cell, which was number one, the officers started the other way round. So they obviously had a plan. The food was given to you in a plastic tray, to keep it warm. My door opened and crash, this guy is trying to attack me, but the tray is in between him and me so I held onto it. In the end they just wrapped me up and put me in the block.

The block or segregation is a small amount of cells away from the main population and is designed as a punishment of isolation and intimidation in order to get you to do what they want you to do. Therefore, they will put you in there for weeks, sometimes months at a time, if it suits their purpose. I was down there on this particular occasion for about two weeks and then the same alleged IRA commander told the governor that he thought Smith had had enough. Now, low and behold, I was back on the wing. The lads said: 'You've got him to thank' so I went and thanked him. He was a very cool guy steeped in history and knowledge of himself which gave him power.

Chapter 10

On trial

My trial for the crimes that I got convicted for ended with sentences which added up to 67 years in total, but running concurrently (which means side-by-side) I ended up with 25 years.

There was very little evidence involved in my case and back in 1995/96 the law was totally different to now, meaning back then you had a 50-50 chance of getting a not guilty if you were innocent. Now it is stacked against you in a way which is unbelievably weighted towards the side of the prosecution.

So there I was, with the co-defendant who had decided that he was going to inform on me to the police. Because of this, he got put in a lower security category prison; however, on the day of the actual trial he was in the court cell with me. In the same cell there were a few good IRA guys who were on trial at the Old Bailey at the same time, and basically the commander of the three told my co-d in no uncertain terms that he was a proven rat and they had seen it for themselves in black and white. He then rang the alarm bell and the officers took him out of the cell and he went into a single.

The way they managed to get the trial together against me and secure the conviction was by saying that the same gun was used in all five offences that I was charged with and, if it was the same gun, it must be the same gunman. But this was total nonsense because all the crimes were in different places at different times, and they had different descriptions of different people who had supposedly committed them. So, if I had had five individual trials for the five offences, I am positive I would have been found not guilty. But they decided to put all five offences together: the attempted murder of two police officers; possession of firearms (which to this day have never been shown to any court); armed robbery of a jewellers, escape from custody and another shooting of a person who was in the wrong place at the wrong time. They then said that due to the fact that it was the same gun - which they did not even have - they were going to try everything together.

I had a QC by the name of Lawrence Kershen. He was competent, but now, when I look back at it, I suppose he probably thought in the back of his mind – and rightly so - that I needed to be in prison. Therefore, he tried without really trying.

On the other hand, my co-d had a very good QC by the name of William Clegg and I must admit he did a good job for him, even though it was much easier and more straightforward because of the fact that he was a rat.

And so the trial commenced and I've got a hostile co-defendant next to me with all of his fans in the public gallery taking the piss out of me like all of a sudden they are bad because I'm in a cage.

So then they proceeded to start bringing in the witnesses to give their evidence. Most of them were behind a screen so we could not see each other because they were claiming that they were scared. And then the police did their part by adding lots of armed guards everywhere, which has a very powerful psychological effect on the jury, because they automatically assume that you must be dangerous for all those police to be there.

The judge's name was Mr Lowry, a wily old fox well-seasoned in the game of locking people up. At one point, one of the police officers deliberately, but obviously pretending not to, said something to the jury that he was not meant to disclose; under normal circumstances that would be enough for you to have a retrial. Mr Lowry, when challenged with this, said that it was a storm in a teacup and started laughing at his own joke.

Then they played the tape of my co-d's statement. Not only did he make a verbal one, he actually took them to every single place we went to on that night and, where he could remember, provided the name of the person where we stopped. At that time, in that world, this was a mortal sin and a no-no. Even up until today, this holds true for some, although 20 years on most people don't really care about principles and everybody is just chasing money and they don't care if it comes from Scotland Yard straight into their bank account.

So, once a tape of that nature is played it is very poignant. He was saying stuff like 'He put the gun in my waist and jammed me with it and said "Get on the fucking bike! Get on the fucking bike!" and then fired a shot into the air.' Therefore, his life was in danger and he had to do what he was told, and that's why he helped me escape from the scene of the crime. Between him and their star witness, who was behind the screen telling the jury, that in a letter that the police found, in which she was confessing to being a full-blown crackhead, it was actually weed she was talking about. Well, I've seen a lot of things in my days but I have never seen white weed. Say no more.

So after all of the theatre, I got found guilty, and the ironic thing is that the only not guilty that I received was for the shooting of another black man. Remember that the prosecution claimed that if it was the same gun, then it must be same gunman. Therefore, one would assume I would be guilty of everything or nothing if you went by their pretexts of how the law should be applied. That black man in question I genuinely don't know him, or his name. What I do know is what was in the statements that he made about the incident that happened to him.

He claimed that he was standing in a stairwell and a young black male with wild-looking eyes told him to come off the stairwell. Five minutes later the same person was coming back down the stairs and challenged him about not getting out of the stairwell, and then apparently shot him in his leg when things got heated. At the time when he told that story to the police they mocked him, and called him a liar and a crackhead, basically jogged him on. I don't even think they called an ambulance. Six months later, however, once it transpired that this person who said he got shot, might have got shot by the same person that shot two police officers, they sent the police to him and basically kissed his arse, telling him how sorry they were, promising him the world just to make a statement, in order to entangle me tighter inside the net. He went along with it, but for his troubles justice did not apply to him. Justice is whatever the powers that be say it is, so to you my black brother, even though I genuinely do not know you, I hope and wish that if you are still alive your life is decent and you are comfortable and content inside your heart and I hold no feelings whatsoever towards your misguided anger at whoever shot you.

My co-defendant was found not guilty and took great glee in smirking at me. While on the subject of this person, it so happened that 20 years later, by fluke, I parked my car at the back of a McDonald's and went through an alleyway to the main road to buy something, and there I saw this guy. I would have just kept on walking but he decided that he was gonna huff and puff and make a commotion on the roadside when police are driving about, and to make it worse it was Eid and he was in the full kameez and prayer cap. Now this is a perfect example of the kind of confused people that are in certain parts of our society. But just like all of us, he can only answer to God for his own sins, just like I will have to answer for mine. At least I am trying to atone myself, while keeping it real at the same time. If you cannot be real and true to yourself, you cannot be real in anything you do.

When the big day came for the sentencing, the courthouse was full of police; the public gallery on my part was empty because I told people to stay away, but there was one person there, somebody who I had known from school days and who had pretended to like me as a person and to be my friend. Funny thing is, in the year before my sentencing I had seen that man's face maybe once, twice tops, but lo and behold, on the day of my sentencing, this man has found all his ID and was willing to show it to the police just in order to be able to sit in that public gallery and watch me get sentenced. This to me shows your true colours and I hope you enjoyed the spectacle and it enriched your life.

Judge Lowry did not waste too much time in dispatching me. He gave me 67 years in total and stated how dreadful crimes must receive dreadful sentences and he could not foresee any time in the future when there would ever be anything positive for or about me. In other words, he gave me that sentence, thinking that he was destroying me as I would not be able to complete it. But the opposite has happened and I have served my sentence and now I'm in the process of redeeming my own self and looking into my own self, understanding my own self, so I can give back something to the people that are closest to my heart - poor, underprivileged people, living every day in pain.

So, in giving me a fixed sentence instead of a life sentence, he unwittingly gave me the opportunity to be sitting here telling my story, which every word of it is the truth. It's very hard for people to be told the truth, especially about themselves, but I have reached the stage where the truth and getting the truth to as many people as possible, in whatever narrative possible, is the only thing that matters.

Understanding the system

As I said at the beginning, the court system is drastically changed since I was on trial. As you can see the title of this book is 'Out of the Box'. Therefore, as the reader you can draw from it what you will and what you do with that knowledge is your business.

So moving on to today's court system, they now have a lot of laws which are solely there to lock you up. The average policeman does not think you are innocent of anything, and once he has you in a position where he can put you into prison that will be his sole goal. You're not even a human being in his eyes; you are a subject or a target.

When they say that if you do not make a statement when you are arrested it may go against you in court, this is nonsense. Once you do get to court, the only thing that will matter will be the 12 people in that jury box and whether they believe you or not. Unfortunately, most people who go on trial for violent crimes have already got criminal records and they choose to try to hide this from the jury, which puts you in a position where you cannot call any member of the prosecution a liar, otherwise they will be entitled to give the jury your criminal record past and that's it. Game over. Now they have managed to make you seem like a liar, for the simple fact that you tried to deceive the jury, so my advice would be, where possible, to tell the truth as far as past convictions are concerned.

They now also say that you have to produce a written defence statement 90 days or so before the actual trial. This is so they know what you're saying, or what your defence is, but I assure you that you will not see all of your prosecution paperwork until maybe the day before the trial date and they will always come out with one piece of evidence which they have held back, and which nine times out of ten, will not be factored into the statement that you made three months prior. At this stage you're already in prison. The only people who matter to you are the jury, therefore you do not have to pander to the prosecution, because if you give your statement after they have given all of theirs to you, the probability of justice becomes in your favour. Yes, you do this at the price of upsetting the judge and the prosecutor, but they are not your friends anyway, so therefore it should make no difference to you, because it makes no difference to the judge when he's given 35 years to people who did not do the crime.

If you are in prison awaiting trial your whole life will be on a knife edge. One way lies total disaster and the other way there is an opportunity for you. So you would be prudent to spend your time in the library and around people of knowledge, in order to grasp as much as you can, as fast as you can, for that big day, because once you are in there that day they will be coming and it's for you to be ready not anybody else. As I said before, none of this really pays but some people learn things the hard way, and therefore I'm trying to give you both sides.

The last thing on this matter is that if you are made Category A and you go on any visit, legal or social, inside the high security system, be advised that those visits might be bugged. These are facts and at one point there was even a scandal in Woodhill prison because they actually did it to the MP Sadiq Khan, who is now London mayor, and who was visiting a prisoner there. I personally know at least 10 people who have been convicted from recordings covertly made on visits, so there you go - you have been warned.

At the time I'm writing this book, one of the terrible old laws has just come under a welcome attack from the senior judges in the Supreme Court and it now seems like this joint enterprise law, which has a lot of people in prison, has been partially overturned. Half of the people locked up for joint enterprise just probably went out for a night out with friends, and one person decided to get into a fight and someone's been stabbed or shot, and everybody who went out that night with that individual has been charged with murder. And unless you're planning to tell it as it is, if you are a straight goer you will be getting life, just like the person that actually committed the crime. Hopefully this law has now been overturned, as a lot of innocent people didn't deserve a life sentence.

Fighting such convictions still isn't easy, and nor is maintaining your human rights in prison. Thanks in particular to MP Mr Grayling the rights of a prisoner now come down to who you know and how much money they've got access to, because that man Mr Grayling decided to take away nearly all legal aid concerning prison issues. In other words, giving all power over to the prison officers, unless you personally know how to navigate the system and take cases to the County Court etc. Otherwise you will never have a chance now and no solicitor will be interested, because there is no money involved any more.

Grayling also did a lot of other negative things and sometimes I wonder why. Maybe it's just that he felt the need to have his name stamped on stuff while he had that short period in office controlling prisons. But whatever the reason, none of it really makes any sense.

Chapter 11

Golden Brown

Heroin is a brown substance - an opiate that acts as a painkiller to the human body. It is widely regarded as a drug of choice for underprivileged white people. Whilst growing up in South London in a black circle that was on the fringes of Jamaican circles, heroin was a drug that I would never come across. Therefore, what it was and what it actually did to one's body was new to me. All I know is that the first time I tried it, it knocked me out and made me sleep like a baby.

Looking back at it now, I can see why or how I immersed myself into a continuous state of heroin-induced slumber and at the time it suited me fine. I had just been given 25 years' imprisonment and I did not feel in my heart that I could do this with a straight head.

At that time in the late 1990s, inside the high security dispersal prison system more than half of the white Cockney gangster type prisoners were using heroin, but only a few among the black inmates were. So, this was not the norm and it was frowned upon, and rightly so.

So here I am in Full Sutton, surrounded by people who had been in there for years and years, some for decades, and they were all warped and twisted in their own right, violent and with their own rules of conduct. To tell the truth, up to that point I'd never seen anything like it.

Then you add in the drug barons who would give you heroin credit, depending on how much money you were worth outside. Some people ran up tabs for £1,100 or £1,300 per month on a regular basis. It got so bad that on one occasion two inmates who were in debt to the tune of £2,000 decided that they were gonna rob the canteen. Yes, I kid you not. There were three of them, and two of them managed to get in through the small hole at the front of the canteen shop and they open the door for the third man, but a prison officer saw them, so the third man grabbed some phone cards, a few thousand pounds worth, and hightailed it back to the wing. Then the officer pressed the alarm and before you know it there's a siege and the two inmates have got the canteen staff at knifepoint, demanding medication for their withdrawal symptoms. They did get medication, but they also got seven years for their troubles.

This is what the place was like. Another guy, who is dead

now, so I can actually name him, was Fred Lowe. He was inside for murder and was a murderous individual that the outside world had forgotten. The time came in Long Lartin when he was on the same wing as some Cockney gangsters and one of them, who is now also dead, took offence over some black kid who kept singing loud music all night. The Cockneys warned him but he kept doing it. He was only doing a small sentence and by any account was a simple guy. In any case, the Cockneys told Fred to stab him up and for that this he would get his debt wiped, so he would not owe the £500 or whatever it was that he owed at the time. So Lowe, being psychotic, went into the man's cell and stabbed him up, then cut his two wrists and left the man for dead. And he did die. That's prison for you - dead with just a few months left to go home just because he wanted to sing to himself at night in his own cell.

In those times the IRA were at the top of the pecking order, then the Cockneys and a small scattering of black guys. In general, it was a free-for-all; there was no real co-ordinated order and the prison officers used to be seen and not heard. You only went to work if you felt like it and apart from that you were left on your own to your own devices. I remember these times as being a long rebellious haze full of pain, with cannabis and that nasty drug to numb it. I personally did not experience some of the stigma that other people got for taking heroin, but obviously you know the environment where you are; people become naturally bitter and twisted and they will murder your name behind your back. This is part and parcel of taking Class A drugs. Sometimes I used to wonder and say to myself: 'Look what your life's come to', but the thought of standing tall on that 25 years was bigger than me at the time and I'm man enough to admit it. In a weird way it took me full circle and now I'm much humbler and my outlook on life is much more realistic because I've let go of my ego.

On the flipside, I have seen people who are in prison buy a house outside from the proceeds of heroin dealing inside prison. They started off with just one ounce or £700 and the house that they bought was a one-bedroom flat for £97,000. This is what can happen behind bars if you do not take drugs yourself.

After about eight years, I started taking opiate-based painkillers which act the same as heroin and therefore take away the urge or need to take heroin. That remains my situation up to today, and right now I am the poor equivalent of Michael Jackson or Prince with prescription painkillers.

I'm happy to see that most kids nowadays do not need to be told never to take drugs, any form of Class A drugs - coke, heroin, LSD, ecstasy - they are all bad for your body and mind. Cannabis - not skunk but Jamaican cannabis - is the only thing you should ever need. That will give you a high and a nice meditation and make you feel hungry, so you wanna eat and stay healthy. The rest is not for you. Please never take drugs. They will get the better of you within time, whether you like it or not.

Ironically, it is Islam that swept through the high security estate and got rid of the majority of Class A drugs inside the establishments. The reason is that if you are a practising Muslim you would never take drugs, and because now most of the inmates are Muslim, there are fewer people trying to bring drugs in to the prison and fewer people willing to buy them. I would not pretend that this was all achieved with kid gloves because it was not. Prison is a violent place where the most organised violent forces rule and this can pan out in all kinds of ways. For example, be a prominent gunman in your own right in your own area, get 20 years for a shooting, then get into the high security estate and realise that the person you shot was a Muslim, or has friends in the prison, and now you have got a problem that is bigger than you, even if your name is Superman, because someone will just come out of the woodwork and stab you up. After you've been stabbed up you will have a choice to become a Muslim and do your 20 years in peace, and so it goes on. Eventually a small percentage of people who became Muslim in these dubious circumstances might still end up thinking it was the best thing that ever happened to them in their life, but the rest will have to hide their feelings away until their last day there and I have seen many a wannabe bad man crumble inside that place.

Chapter 12

The Deen

Top-security UK prison where terror fanatics serve life sentences is 'al-Qaeda recruiting centre'

21:01, 29 MAR 2014

BY NICK DORMAN , SEAN RAYMENT - THE SUNDAY PEOPLE

At category A Whitemoor jail an astonishing 42 per cent of convicts follow the Islamic faith - a figure in stark contrast to the overall UK population of just 5%

Risk: Zia Al Haq (above left) and Nezal Hindawi are both serving at Whitemoor

A top-security prison where almost half the inmates are Muslims is a breeding ground for Islamic extremists, experts warned last night.

The Sunday People reveals that category A Whitemoor jail, where terror fanatics are serving life sentences for plotting mass murder in the UK, is a recruiting centre for al Qaeda, according to alarmed staff, prison inspectors and politicians.

An astonishing 42 per cent of convicts at the prison near March, Cambs, follow the Islamic faith.

The figure is in stark contrast to the overall UK population in which just five per cent are Muslim.

Violent jihadists in Whitemoor are recruiting vulnerable inmates, pressurising them into converting to Islam before joining terrorist groups, the Government has been warned.

One prison officers' union source said: "Whitemoor is now effectively run by Muslims, many of whom are Jihadis."

Other top-security prisons are not far behind, with 33 per cent Muslim inmates at Belmarsh in south-east London and 20 per cent at Full Sutton near York and Long Lartin, Worcs.

Last night Labour's shadow justice secretary Sadiq Khan told the Sunday People: "The Government hasn't even noticed these alarming figures.

"While the Justice Secretary is busy with gimmicks he has no idea if and to what extent radicalisation is taking place in our prisons.

"The Government has failed to take action on this. In jails like Whitemoor the Chief Inspector is on record warning of the risks of radicalisation.

"The Government needs to wake up to this problem before it's too late."

The first time I ever came across a Muslim prisoner was in the late 1990s, around 1997 or so; he went by the name of Hindawi and he was doing a very long sentence for terrorism. At the time I did not really understand or care to know more than that outline of his scenario, mainly because I was too consumed with my own issues, ie taking hard drugs. Therefore, at the time that was the only thing that mattered to me. But now, with 20 years' insight I can understand a bit more how he got to be in prison thousands of miles away from Palestine. A lot of people thought he was evil but just like the IRA prisoners he had his own brothers' and sisters' blessing and his gripe was - or is if he is still alive - political.

In any setting, if there is only a very small number of one set of people, they can easily go unnoticed. At that time, in 1997, the main body of prisoners at the top were IRA members or Cockney gangster type people, and then you had the other mixture of people who were robbers, killers, gunmen and what have you. Around 2000, I started going to prayers on a Friday. At this stage, there were only a handful of people who used to go there, and people were there for all different reasons - the people who wanted to pray were at the front with the rest at the back. This went on for a long while, then all of the IRA prisoners went back to Ireland and slowly there was a shift and more and more brothers started coming to prison.

Now I must stop here to remind you that prison is a cage. Therefore, the only thing that matters, if you wish to control the whole system, is numbers. Ironically, faith or deep belief or conviction can bring you solitude and peace within, which in itself can be very appealing to anybody in a cage. Things continued in this vein, but slowly more and more brothers, or inmates that were brothers, were coming into the prison. Then around 2005 Sheikh Faisal came to the prison on terrorism charges, but in reality all he had been doing was speaking his mind, based on the facts as he saw it. I met him when he came to Long Lartin and I liked him. He was a Jamaican and very, very clever, with a wide range of political and religious knowledge from all round the world; he spoke Arabic and knew the Quran by heart. He used to get into arguments with other prisoners who were way less enlightened than him - and that's putting it politely. When they could not win their argument verbally, they would want to resort to violence and on more than a few occasions I had to jump in and stop it and then I would say to people things like 'If you can't beat the man with an intellectual argument, then don't talk to him, but do not turn around and try to use violence because you know that your argument is weak.'

Then you had a lot of other prisoners, mostly white guys or guys who had power up until this point and who could see how they could lose it because of this new influx of prisoners, so they would take every opportunity to cast Muslims in a bad light. From the mere fact that a Muslim prisoner did not need drugs or drink to function inside the prison system and only needed food and exercise in the gym, it was clear from the start that brothers could adapt to anything. Slowly but surely inmates started to convert, some for inner peace, others for their own ends, or to seek personal power. That category of person is only fooling themselves. Brothers used to always come up to me and try to convert me but, because I believe in my heart that God is not a joke, I did not jump on the bandwagon for the sake of it.

Mr Haq, the other brother in the article about Whitemoor is a brother I also know, due to the fact we were on the same landing, and I found him to be polite, courteous, intelligent and genuine. I personally would trust or take his word, over any politician that I have seen or met in my life time.

The dispersal prison system has always been a violent place, from the 1980s all the way up to now, but now with the introduction of larger numbers of Muslim prisoners, it put the brothers in a strong position and by 2007 they were the strongest force in the high security prison system. Once a number becomes over 51 per cent inside a prison, the other 49 will follow. This is Maths. Islam is all about peace and a wholesome way of living your life, and that had a great appeal to a lot of people who are in the midst of extreme turmoil caused both by their own actions and the brutality of the system. As a result of this, things which people had been doing before, such as taking a shower naked without your boxer shorts began to get you into trouble for not conforming to the new social norm. Myself, I do think people should wear them in there but if you were some hillbilly farm boy doing your bird you're not gonna like being told, and most of the guys who were previously at the top of the pecking order were now walking on egg shells.

Understanding history

Since Islam became national news and the topic of so much attention, a lot of things have been said by a lot of different people for lots of different reasons - mostly money; and then people will harp on about how 'Muslims have taken over our prisons', but nobody seems to have the common sense to start from the beginning. If you do that then you will come to a better understanding of what's going on. The IRA are gone and the facts are that one person's terrorist is another person's freedom fighter and these are the feelings which people have problems understanding and accepting.

So now we go back to the beginning. A historian can go back thousands of years, but I'm just a normal guy who took a journey which most people don't take, and I can only tell you how I see it from my perspective, which is based on common sense and facts.

A hundred years ago, there was a very famous British soldier by the name of Lawrence of Arabia, and his job was to go on behalf of Britain to what we now know as Saudi Arabia and convince the Bedouin Arabs that they should fight for them, ie the British and French, because they were the only people who can live in that terrain. He mixed with the Arabs, smoked their peace pipe, drank their coffee, pretended to be a brother or equal and promised them the world. The Bedouin Arabs, being honourable people in their own right, did battle with the Ottomans and came out on top. Therefore, England and France's dirty work had been completed by a third party. These are all documented facts which are undeniable. Once the battle was over, England and France secretly made an agreement with each other, not to honour the agreement made originally, but to carve up all the Arab lands into spheres of influence, over which the two countries would preside. They gave the Bedouin

Arabs the part left over, which just consisted of miles and miles of sand. Yes, barren desert sand - and I personally could imagine the person in charge of this finding it very amusing because of his status, social circle and deluded belief that he was better. And then, lo and behold, not even 40 years later it was discovered that there were trillions and trillions of dollars, pounds, euros or francs worth of oil under that very same desert.

This in itself would show a wise person that no man rules the cycle of life or the world, and that everything on and in it, is only for a time. So now what happens? They do the next best thing, which they are extremely good at and show 50,000 different faces for 50,000 different people. They go back to the Arabs in what is now Saudi Arabia and befriend them in order to buy the very same oil which they did not know existed when they gave away the desert. These are the ironies of life. Nobody but God can control them. After Saudi Arabia was established, from then on dark forces would always be in the background trying to control it.

Most people don't know this part of the history of western powers and the Muslim world, but one thing which lots and lots of people do know and identify with, is Palestine. The making of the state of Israel is another of Britain's crimes – they got that land for the Zionists, not because they cared about Jewish people escaping from the Nazis but, as with everything else they do, in order to control the area and plunder its oil and natural resources. Israel has committed some of the world's worst atrocities against the Palestinian people and lots of people around the world, especially those who are themselves oppressed, identify very strongly with the Palestinians' struggle for freedom and justice. Some people show their support by going on demonstrations and boycotting certain shops and foods; others take a more direct approach to supporting what is, after all, an armed struggle.

And coming up to date, there is also the question of what Britain did in Iraq from 2003 to now. The leader of our country at the time clearly said to the world that Saddam Hussein - who by the way had been Britain's ally at one point - had weapons of mass destruction, which could reach England within 45 minutes. As we all know, this was a total and complete lie. So now these odd individuals with their 50,000 faces, who you invest your trust in and who you vote for, gave us another war. Not to mention Afghanistan.

If you were from Afghanistan or Iraq and your family was destroyed along with your house, your shops and everything you have, how would you feel really? Or do you feel it doesn't concern you, because it's not happening to you'

Dr Bilal

'Doctor by day, terrorist by night' and 'a new breed of British terrorist' is how the British papers described Dr Bilal Abdulla in 2008, when he went on trial for planning bomb attacks in London and Glasgow. It's another example of the same negative narrative that is directed from the top down, showing Muslims in general in a bad light. The everyday public grab onto the negatives without really understanding what is going on around them and who is the real orchestrator of this vicious cycle, which in all probability is not going to end the way that the orchestrator planned.

Dr Bilal, when I met him in Belmarsh, Frankland and other prisons, came across as articulate caring and sincere, a well-read person of higher education and understanding. He was from Iraq and had seen his country destroyed and had lost members of his family to a war that nobody over there had asked for. It was Britain and the USA that dropped the bombs and created carnage and destruction, but the powers-that-be ignored this and just focussed on the acts he was charged with. This is the confused twisted back-to-front mindset they would like you to buy into. After all, even the thickest of persons would understand that in order to understand something properly you would have to start from the beginning. They refuse to do this because they know they know where it would lead back to.

And where do people whose countries are being wrecked by the imperialists go to? They've been living there for thousands of years. Move on to Syria, as it is at the moment in the middle of war. Do you honestly believe that everybody in Syria just woke up one day and said we would like to live like English people, so we will leave here and go to England, where we will be free? (This incidentally is the opposite of the truth because you are not free in England unless you've got money.) No, that was not the case; instead the same dark forces trying to control everything in the region, unwittingly - and presumably not intentionally - opened a Pandora's Box that they can't close, and now there are thousands and thousands of people trying to get to safety and little babies drowning in seas and rivers. And by safety, they mean countries like Britain, whose own leaders are the ones really responsible for their plight.

I personally have met some of the strongest, most decent and honourable human beings in prison who I have ever met in my life, and I don't have a bad word to say about them. As for the younger brothers with less education, just like me, if you don't know something, then somebody wiser does. Don't let frustration and everything else that prison consists of, keep you in a constant state of anger.

I appreciate that a lot of young guys aren't gonna really be listening too much and have their own way of looking at things, but all I can say to you is, don't sit down and take 20 years to learn something you can learn in ten, just because you are too hard-headed to listen in the first place. When you come across people who you have tried to show Deen and they do not want to know, that is between them and God. You haven't got a right to be judge, jury and executioner. And because I'm real, I'm going to call you out on this, because it's wrong and gives brothers a bad name unnecessarily. There are no stripes for victimising the weak.

A lot of this comes down to age and education; in the real world outside of prison there are brothers who will walk past you and never even acknowledge you, no matter what comes out of your mouth. These are all realities, so one would be wise to put things in perspective, ie your surroundings, the nature of the people who have got you in that cage and so on. Unless you do this, you will have problems and may end up in a unit somewhere, like some other guys have done. Nobody is tougher than the prison bars. You can wear a £50,000 watch and have £10,000 in your prison private cash account, but in reality you are deluded, because in prison there is only one thing that matters, and that is getting out honourably and in one piece.

Chapter 13

A cage is a violent place

In this chapter, I am going to tell you two true stories to try to give you a feel of the atmosphere in the high security estate prison. These dramas are played out every day, every week, every month, every year, adding to the actual punishment of being in prison, which is meant to be the loss of liberty retribution, rehabilitation and then reallocation into society.

The first scenario involved a man I have known since the 1990s. His name is Dwain. He is dark skinned, slim and athletic, very violent and eager to commit violent acts. When I first met him he was serving 13 years for robberies and he served all of it. He got released and within nine months was back in prison for two murders and several armed robberies. Upon his return I met back up with him at Belmarsh, where I was on accumulated visits. This is where you come from a prison in the countryside to one in London, so your visitors can come to see you. So he was on the exercise yard in a yellow and blue prison tracksuit, which is allocated to people who have escaped or attempted to escape. I greeted him and asked him about the tracksuit, and he told me that he had set the prison bus alight in order for them to stop the van, so he could escape, but the officers took him to a secure building and overpowered him. This is the character I'm talking about.

Two days later the officer told him to go in his cell and he turned around and knocked him out. When he eventually went to court for all his new offences, he was given four life sentences, one for murder and the rest for robberies. When you get a man like this in a cage where there's nowhere to go there can only be one outcome eventually, but when it's right in front of you and the outcome is all around you, it is not a nice scenario to be in.

So Dwain gets moved from prison to prison for assaults. Sometimes it was for himself over some perceived disrespect; at other times it was for money paid by other people who did not have the heart to do things themselves. So it was only a matter of time before some of his victims would be Muslim prisoners and they would be playing by a different game, which is what makes that place so dangerous, because the person who offered you a plate of food to eat yesterday could be the same person who is going to stab you or cut your throat today. I have seen scenarios like that played out real-life, real-time.

Anyway, at some stage Dwain got involved in a stand-off with the prison officers and all of the prisoners were meant to sit outside and refuse to go behind their cell doors, in protest at certain issues that had arisen. One inmate decided that he was not going to take part in this and went to go behind his cell door. Dwain took offence to this and promptly broke the brother's jaw. Personally I don't agree with this and did not at the time, because that inmate was very polite, never troubled anybody and was physically small in height and body mass, so there was no need for it.

This was the beginning of the end for Dwain, because after that scenario he was moved to HMP Whitemoor, and by then his victims had started to more than multiply, and there was a brother who was very physical and soon for release who seemed hell-bent on getting released with a big buzz around his name as a hard man or a good brother, depending on what way you look at it.

So this brother decides that he's heard so much about Dwain that he would be the person to bring Dwain's reign to an end. It so happened that I had landed in Whitemoor a few weeks before Dwain. When I saw him come on the landing I thought to myself 'wrong place, wrong time' and advised him to be careful. The very next day, when he went to the gym, four brothers tried to smash an iron weights pole over his head, but luckily for him, at that time there was somebody else there who knew everybody and who could get in the middle and that's what saved his life on that day.

After that they put Dwain in segregation and again I ended up down there, serving 14 days' solitary confinement for failing a drugs test. Everybody was talking out of the cell windows and then on one occasion I got a chance to speak to Dwain on his own on the exercise yard and I advised him again to leave the prison and change his ways. I went back up onto the wing after this and then about a week later I got the news. Everyone on the whole wing was talking and putting their two pence worth in so I asked somebody what was going on and they told me.

Apparently, a sadistic security governor, who knew full well that Dwain was in very hot water and should have been moved to another prison, instead of doing his job like a professional, decided to offer Dwain the opportunity to relocate onto the very landing where all of the people that wanted to kill him were housed, knowing full well that, Dwain being Dwain, would have too much pride and heart not to go. As the narrative inside these places is one of 'us against them', you do not want them to think that you need their protection or indeed for anybody inside the arena to believe that you need protection. This is perceived as being weak. So he took the bait and went up onto the landing and, from all accounts, he came close to death more than once that night and had to be taken to outside hospital for multiple fractures to his skull. Basically he is now only 40% of his normal self at best, and will never be the same again. These are the kind of dramas that get played out.

Dirty Dread

This second scenario is a continuation from the Dwain scenario, but this time one of the two characters is me. I will endeavour to tell the story to the best of my ability and factoring in the time span. The person that I had an altercation with is a Jamaican and at the time and for many years before and after he did have locks, so I will call him the Dirty Dread (no disrespect intended to true Rastas). For a Jamaican he was unusual, because he was large in structure and physical, which in a Jamaican is an unusual combination. He was serving a life sentence for a murder that he did not commit. But he was a character that lived his life that way and came to England in the late 1990s, where he was hanging around with a friend of mine who is now dead. RIP.

Therefore, by time I actually met Dirty Dread, we already had common ground and, to be honest, for a year or so we were fine and on a few occasions he did back me up in scenarios, most of which I had caused myself down to taking drugs, but eventually we just went off each other and dislike led onto hate. At first it was on the back of no real incident, then a group of guys came into the dispersal system from South London, young, fresh guys, with fresh stories and money and charisma to match, and I ended up around them. We just clicked and for some reason the Dirty Dread did not really like one of the guys. There were three of them: the second one was neutral and the third one Dirty Dread was definitely afraid of at this time.

In Full Sutton high security prison you are allowed to cook your own food. Therefore, that is the highlight of the day, and on the weekends people go all out and have big meals. At the time the wing that I was on had two main black circles and Dirty Dread's one was bigger than the other one, which I will just say was mine for argument's sake, but in reality was just the circle that I have already mentioned. So on the day in question, which was a Sunday, we decided to make a big meal and invite the inmates that we liked to eat with us and we proceeded to cook food. The wing was laid out with two tables on each section and lots of chairs, and people just used the tables and chairs as they needed, so when it was time for us to start sharing our food, I decided to put the two tables together so we could all eat as one. One of the tables was dirty, so I cleaned it.

Two minutes later, who turns up but Dirty Dread saying 'You can't have both of the tables' and all sorts of nonsense, because in reality what he wants to do is create a situation. So he proceeded to pull one of the tables onto the other side of the landing. At that point I said to myself 'Fuck this' and went to the dustbin that had the rubbish in that I had originally cleaned from the table and proceeded to pour it all over the table, telling him that that was how I found it.

This made him madder and, before you know, it people are running around the table, escalating the situation and saying what they are going to do. I'm a cautious person, so if you say to me, you're going to do something to me, I will definitely get you first. The best line of defence is attack.

Anyway, the situation got calmed down, due to the fact that it was going to be lock-up time. So that night, before we got locked up, we made a quick plan and first thing in the morning, before going to work, we finalised it. The plan was for me to stab Dirty Dread in his neck in the workshop. The workshop was a large working area with about 50 inmates working in there at any one time, with long screwdrivers, scissors, all sorts of tools, and about three prison officers tops, there at any one time.

Looking back, I can laugh at this now but at the time it really, really wasn't funny because Dirty Dread surpassed himself that day. I had heard stories about how mad he got when his own blood was drawn, but on that day I was going to see for myself first hand. So we are in the workshop: me, the guy from South London that he hates and our big friend from North London - and when I say big, I mean in size, but with a big beautiful heart to go with it. So the plan was for me to just run up to him and stab him in his neck and then run past, where our big friend would get in his way and block his path, and we believed that by then it would all be over, because the alarm bell would have gone off and when this happens every available officer runs to the scene. So I'm sitting there thinking that I'd better get this timing right and also that I'd better not make him get into a situation where he could actually grab hold of me. And that was it. I just jumped up, ran over to him from the side and proceeded to push this ice pick through his neck.

But it did not work. I believe because of the locks and a big beard, the ice pick went across at the wrong angle and did not find its mark. He spun around and went past my big friend, who was meant to jump up and block Dirty Dread's path to me. The man was like a raging bull with a screwdriver in his hand and the only thing between me and certain death was a very large table made out of wood. So every time he tried to come around it, I would just do the same thing. Our big friend by then had jumped up and tried to block him, but he was so mad by now that he stabbed my big friend and they had a little fast, violent skirmish.

By now the bell had gone off, but the officers who were in the workshop were too scared to jump in without their friends for back-up, so there's Dirty Dread still trying to kill me, and by time the officers did come there was about 60 of them. They tried to handcuff me first but I was like: 'No fucking way - handcuff that nigger first!'

We were both taken to segregation and I was shipped out of the prison and he was put back on the wing. Then maybe a year or so after, another inmate of influence squashed it all, and Dirty Dread agreed. So a good few years went past with us on talking terms, even if there was no love lost. Then some four years later, the man used an incident, that had nothing to do with him whatsoever, to punch me in my face.

These are the kind of scenarios that get played out daily, weekly, yearly in prison. That last violation is one of the very few times in my life that someone had done that, and I decided that it was prudent and wise to leave it be, because he was doing life and therefore did not have a release date. My release date was less than two years away at the time and, considering I had been in the segregation unit, over a 15-year period, at least 20 times accused of stabbing people, I did not want to push my luck. I had a sneaky feeling that it would be just my luck that, on this occasion, something would stick for my 25-year sentence to get changed to a life sentence without a release date. I've seen this happen to other prisoners who couldn't control their anger and were more concerned about what other people have done to them than about their own future.

I hear that Dirty Dread did manage to get deported back to Jamaica and is now a free man, so the chances are he will read this and know I am talking about him. So if you ever read this, all I want to say to you is: 'Hope you put that psychology degree to good use Dirty Dread.'

I hope these two stories have given you an insight into the parallel worlds that run alongside the outside 'real' world.

Wasteman – wasting away...

'You're a wasteman, wasting away wasting away.' These were the hooks in the lyrics that one of my friends had made up while serving time in HMP Whitemoor. At the time he was only serving seven years and should not really have even been in such a prison, but he did have a saving grace - he was a good DJ and had a circle of friends who happened to be doing 35 years and who, unlike him, were powerful in the prison, so he always had people that would protect him.

On the day when he made up the lyrics, I knew it was how he was feeling about the atmosphere inside the place and his views towards most of the prisoners, and the raw fact that everybody inside there was actually just wasting away. But to actually say it out the window would take a braver man than me. I told him to listen to my advice and keep it to himself.

Then, a few weeks later, he decided for no real reason that he's going to take his shahada. This in itself is not a joke and should be done for the right reasons, which clearly was not the case on this occasion. Three or four weeks later he got bored, because his heart never was in it in the first place, so he then proceeded to tell the brothers that he did not want to be a brother no more. In their eyes this was very serious and they hated him for it. But once again luckily he had that social circle, so he was able to speak to the right people and pour cold water over everything, and he left the prison in one piece. So to you Mr Wasting Away, I hope you haven't wasted away and I hope that you've put your talents to good use on the outside.

Chapter 14

Freedom of a sort

When you go to prison for more than a decade, you start off after the devastation of being sentenced, in emotional turmoil, and you just blank out the outside world and immerse yourself in your surroundings. But in my case, after 12 years, days started coming to me when I would think about outside and the realisation that time was now working in my favour and the time between then and being released, the time I had left to serve, was becoming less and less.

This builds on you each year that passes, and by the time you get to the last three years, you start getting happy. They call it gate-happy; you are finally gonna get an opportunity to be free!

I was eventually released in 2011. I was collected by my cousin in a brand-new BMW. In the car were a Rolex, an iPhone, £500 and some clothes, as well as a bag full of durex and Chinese Viagra. I remember walking out of Belmarsh and taking in the surreal, peaceful, tranquil surroundings, which were in stark contrast to the disorder that I had just left behind; it was just unbelievable thinking about the things that were going on just behind those walls.

We stopped at McDonald's; then I had to report to the probation in the hostel where I would be living. They proceeded to tell me all the rules and dos and don'ts, and then I was left to my own devices. It was a really nice boiling hot summer, July 2011, and it was just emotional. All the new sights and gadgets, things that did not exist in my time in the 1990s, like Oyster cards, supermarkets where you pay for your stuff yourself to a machine that talks back to you, bendy buses that turn corners and other things. It seemed like all young people were in really expensive cars, and a lot of black people also had really expensive cars. The other most noticeable thing was the amount of people from every different nation of the world; you could go on the train and hear ten different languages, none of them necessarily English. Yeah, it truly was a different world.

The day after my release, I remember walking downstairs in the hostel and going into the garden, where I saw squirrels running around for the first time. It was a bright, hot summer's day and it blew me away.

I met my probation officer. She was a black lady by the name of Julia, very professional, but somebody who I would say had seen a few things in life before becoming a probation officer. In hindsight, I probably let myself get too close to her, or should I say, let my guard down too much; after all she is an officer of the law and her primary function is to analyse you and report to her superiors about you and to liaise with the police at MAPPA meetings. These are meetings for people who the police believe are likely to get into trouble with the law again upon their release.

I then left the hostel and went to a café in an area nearby which seemed very gentrified. I bought a cake and a cup of coffee, and sat down and made a phone call to my grandmother. Upon hearing her voice, I became extremely emotional and just started crying, tears running down my face, and everybody was looking at me like I was strange. I just got up, paid five pounds for the coffee and cake, and left. That is what it was like - a total rollercoaster. I finally got taken to my grandmother's house and this too was another emotional scene with her breaking down and crying, not believing it was really me, after so many years.

My daughter was also with me during the weeks after my release, but that relationship was strained. I became a father when I was just 18 and way too young to be ready to be a good dad.

When all is said and done, I still count myself lucky that

at that time in 2011 there were people around in the background to help me and give me money from time to time. Without that I would have been in complete trouble because, contrary to what David Cameron might have the public believe, once you are released from prison, however long you have served, the most you will end up with is £100 and you have to make your own way.

This is unbelievable but is actually the truth and then people wonder why so many people end up back in prison and it actually costs over £20,000 to house somebody in prison; £40,000 if you're a Category A prisoner, but not a penny in grants or whatever to help you settle in and make a new future after three months in a hostel, which in itself is like a big police station with CCTV cameras everywhere. It is totally monitored and you have to sign a book every night at 11 o'clock to confirm your presence and if you are on curfew you have to be home before your curfew hour has lapsed, otherwise you will end up right back where you started - in prison. So therefore your time in that building is under duress and you have to pander to the staff just to be on the safe side.

And there could be other people inside there who are sex offenders. One guy, an old man, very posh in his mannerisms and very well spoken - apparently he was associated with a lot of well-to-do powerful establishment people - was a serial paedophile and predator. Every other day there would be about five psychologists and all different people, including police, interviewing him and grilling him in the side room and all of the rest of the inmates or ex-inmates, including me, were told that if we were to reveal his identity to any newspapers we would be sent straight back to prison. About two weeks later, the same individual vanished and we were all thinking that he must have left the country or something. Then we got the news that he had jumped on a train-line at Acton station. I can't say there was much sympathy and if I did I would be lying.

Then that Baby P killer came there and the staff were trying to say that we must talk to him and treat him as an equal. I just told them straight that there was no way I was ever going to speak to that man; nor would I be attending any meetings that he would be at. When I did see him he would just put his head down, which suited me fine.

My time at the hostel finally came to an end after five months and I ended up with a flat, which was actually a bedsit, privately rented and paid for by the council. Most people would not feel comfortable in that tiny bedsit but to me, coming from prison, it was nice and I was happy with it, even though it did not belong to me. I decorated it to the best of my ability and installed a CCTV system. Then I applied for my driving test and passed first time, so I got myself a car. It was a black Alfa Romeo.

I also had a special lady and I mean special. She has been a steadfast companion and friend, extremely wise, intellectual, classy and full of finesse. I have no doubt in my mind that if I had not met this person my life would have turned out for the worse again. There definitely would not be a happy ending, and for that I will love and respect her for life. No man is an island; No man stands alone – wise words from the late, great Dennis Brown.

Chapter 15

Back in the clutches of Babylon

The last thing I was expecting at this point was that I'd be going right back to prison nine months later for conspiracy to rob and looking at a life sentence. Yes, life sentence, just like that, but I was all over the place, seeing this one and that one, getting my teeth whitened, going to lap-dance clubs, swingers' clubs, bars and restaurants, and all these things cost money and a lot of money; then I had to also pass my driving test and furnish my flat.

As I take it you all know, it is expensive to live like that, and yes I was getting handouts from people, but as you can imagine nothing lasts forever or is indefinite, apart from death and even that is arguable. So eventually I had to start doing my own thing. I was basically on the fringes of being back to my old ways, but without the firearms, and this continued until the fateful day that I got arrested by heavily armed police.

I ended up getting close to one guy who was staying in the same hostel as me. He was sort of a friend and he had a cousin, Marlon, who had been out for years, had had a long run and was therefore up for anything. Then another guy turned up, that I had known for years from high security prison. There, you would have it; I've got myself a little team.

At this point I would like to interject to you the reader. If by some unfortunate chance you are now in this situation in a hostel reading this book, this is what you do not want to do – in fact, you need to do the opposite of what I did, if you want to have a realistic chance of survival.

So, as I said, I'd got myself a team and we started testing the waters. Nothing great came by way of money, but I was surviving. Then we did end up getting some money, of the sort which most people would say was a decent amount of money to live on for six months at least, but for some reason it wasn't enough for me and I was still running around the streets like it was 1993.

Therefore, it was only a matter of time. Bearing in mind that they only have to get lucky once, but you have to be lucky every day, every week, every month.

Eventually the fateful day came in March 2012. Me and my team were in St John's Wood, and admittedly we had items that could be used to commit robberies, when we were arrested by armed police.

All I can remember is two of my team coming out of the car and then as soon as I and the driver got out, I heard a commotion. As I turned around I was looking down the barrel of an MP5. This policeman was on top of his job and did not come off the gun-sight once, and had that gun trained on me like nobody's business. I put my hands up in one motion and, for a split second, I wondered if he would shoot me. Then he jumped over a car bonnet, landed in front of me and took me down with the butt of his gun.

There were four of them on two of us, doing various different things, like kicking Marlon in the head and jabbing me with the muzzle of the gun, and in the melee one of them said something like: 'You like shooting police, you black bastard? We're going to fucking kill you.'

My reply to this was 'I've done my bird', but it didn't come out in English. Death was all around me and my involuntary fear got the better of me, so when I tried to speak, it was just like the clock stopped and it came out like a squeal. I knew the horrors in front of me if I did not clear my name and get a not guilty. I knew that I would be going to die in there like a dog, while prison officers laughed and joked and read the Sun newspaper and farted and found it humorous. For the first time in my life, I was truly scared. Just the thought of it was enough.

When we got to the police station I made an evaluation of my situation and decided that the only positive thing I could do was go on the record about the fact that I had money in my house. It wasn't the world's biggest sum of money but £3,800 is money if you haven't got any and are about to go to prison. Therefore, once I eventually got processed, I told their sergeant on record about the money that was in my flat, and then again the next day, when my flat had been searched and I was about to be interviewed and it became apparent that the money had not been found by any of the searching officers, I went against legal advice and pointed out on interview about the money and my concerns that the police had stolen it.

RESTRICTED (when complete)

MG 15(T)

RECORD OF INTERVIEW

between 3.79

URN

~~Contemporaneous Notes~~ / ~~SDN~~ / ~~ROTI~~ / ~~ROVI~~ (delete as applicable)

Person interviewed:	Leroy SMITH	Police Exhibit No.	
Place of interview:	Interviewing Room 3, Charring Cross Police Station	Number of Pages	14
		Signature of interviewer producing exhibit	
Date of interview:	15/03/12		
Time commenced:	16:11 pm	Time concluded:	16:33 pm
Duration of interview:	0:22		
Audio tape reference nos.:	T6210767/PMD/4T	Visual image reference nos.:	
Interviewer(s):	DC Dixon / DC Smailes		
Other persons present:	Barbara Sutton (Solicitor)		

Tape counter times	Person speaking	Text
0.12	DC Dixon	Right, this interview is being tape recorded I'm DC Dixon, attached to the Special Projects Team at New Scotland Yard, the other officer present is...
	DC Smailes	Its DC Smailes also attached to the Projects Unit.
	DC Dixon	We're in interview room 3 at Charring Cross Police Station, I'm interviewing Leroy SMITH. Leroy, can you state your name and address for voice association on the tape please?
	Leroy Smith	Leroy Martin SMITH.
	DC Dixon	Thank you. Also present is Leroy's legal representative...
	Solicitor	It's Barbara Sutton from (Inaudible). Can you give me the time DC Dixon...
	DC Dixon	Yeah, sure.
	Solicitor	... I'm without my watch?
0.35	DC Dixon	Yep. Course. The date is the 15th of March, 2012 and the time by my watch is 11 minutes past 4 in the afternoon. This interview is being tape recorded and it may be given in evidence if your case is brought to trial, Leroy.

Signature(s)..

1

2006/07(1): MG 15(T)

RESTRICTED (when complete)

RESTRICTED (when completed) MG 15(T)

erson Interviewed Leroy SMITH

Page 3 of 14

Tape counter times	Person speaking	Text
		your solicitor's already indicated you wish to exercise is. 'You do not have to say anything', alright. So you understand that. 'But it may harm your defence if you do not mention when questioned something which you later rely on in court'.
2.00		Basically, that means if you sit there today and do make 'No comment' in relation to the questions that I ask. When, if this matter were to proceed to court, then a judge may instruct the jury to make some inference from your silence during this interview.
		If you were for example to come up with some version of events at court that you don't come up with today, then they could ask the question, 'Why didn't Leroy say that to the police on the day of his arrest?' Okay.
		The last part of the caution is, 'Anything you do say maybe given in evidence'. As you can see the tapes are in the machine and are recording. And these tapes can be played at court or a transcript can be read out. Alright. Do you understand that?
	Leroy Smith	Yes.
	DC Dixon	Yes. Okay. Right, I've been passed a note from your legal representative...
2.40	Solicitor	Not a note, it's a statement...
	DC Dixon	Sorry, a statement.
	Solicitor	... DC Dixon.
	DC Dixon	Okay. 'I, Leroy SMITH have been arrested for conspiracy to commit robbery. I deny the allegation. I have...
	Solicitor	What, where are you stuck?
	DC Dixon	Oh so; I have not been involved in a conspiracy to, to rob, burgled, steal or commit any kind of criminal offence/activity'.
	Leroy Smith	Yeah.
3.05	DC Dixon	And that's signed L SMITH, date the 15th of March 2012.
		Leroy, can I just ask you just to confirm for the purpose of the tape is that your signature on that note?
	Leroy Smith	Yes.

Signature(s)..
(Contemporaneous notes only)
2004/05(1): MG 15(T)
SP

• Not relevant for contemporaneous notes 3

RESTRICTED (when completed) MG 15(T)

Page 5 of 14

Person Interviewed Leroy SMITH

Tape counter times	Person speaking	Text
		sure I replied, 'I can't answer that; I can't answer that my investigation is un-biased'. Alright. That's a record in relation to the arrest.
4.55	Leroy Smith	It's not true.
	DC Dixon	What's; what's not true? These, these notes aren't right?
	Leroy Smith	They're not right.
	DC Dixon	Okay. What part are you disagreeing with?
	Solicitor	You don't have to go in to go…
	DC Dixon	You don't have to…
	Solicitor	… that now Leroy.
	DC Dixon	Okay.
	Leroy Smith	You made it quite clear.
	DC Dixon	You disagree. Basically you…
5.04	Solicitor	First of all, let me just explain.
	Leroy Smith	I don't sign it.
	Solicitor	You've signed your statement…
	DC Dixon	Okay. No I'm just…
	Solicitor	… Leroy.
	Leroy Smith	Yeah.
	Solicitor	So you've told the officer's, no uncertain terms, not involved in any criminal activity. Yeah, agree with them. That's all you need to do Leroy.
5.12	Leroy Smith	That is true.
	Solicitor	You don't have to discuss any details from (Inaudible)
	Leroy Smith	And the only other thing I wanna say sir, to you is this, yeah. You're supposed to be officers, yeah enforcing the law, yeah, erm, being fine upstanding citizens. So how my money could get stolen from my house…
	Solicitor	Leroy!

Signature(s)………………………………………………………………………………
(Contemporaneous notes only)
2004/05(1): MG 15(T)
SP

• Not relevant for contemporaneous notes

5

RESTRICTED (when completed) MG 15(T)

erson Interviewed Leroy SMITH

Page 6 of 14

Tape counter times	Person speaking	Text
	DC Dixon	Yeah, yeah.
5.28	Leroy Smith	...is beyond me.
	Solicitor	Leroy, we'll discuss that...
	DC Dixon	Leroy, as, what...
	Solicitor	... after the interview.
	DC Dixon	....I'm just gonna explain to you what...
	Leroy Smith	How I can get assaulted...
	DC Dixon	Okay.
	Leroy Smith	... by a gun man, call himself a police officer, yeah when I've got handcuffs on me is beyond me...
5.38	DC Dixon	Okay.
	Leroy Smith	... yeah. The law what you make out to be...
	Solicitor	Okay. Shall we stop...
	DC Dixon	Okay. Okay.
	Solicitor	... and have consultation Leroy?
	Leroy Smith	Yeah. Sorry.
	Solicitor	Or do you want to press on with the interview?
ȷ.45	Leroy Smith	No I don't.
	DC Dixon	Okay.
	Leroy Smith	But it's...
	Solicitor	Okay.
	Leroy Smith	... just unbelievable.
	Solicitor	Well, again, you've serve your statement Leroy and, you know if you want to refer the officer's to that for any other questions, then you can do that...
	Leroy Smith	That's what he needs to do he's, yeah
	Solicitor	Okay.

ignature(s)..
(Contemporaneous notes only)
2004/05(1): MG 15(T)
SP

•Not relevant for contemporaneous notes 6

Once that was on record I did what everybody should do if they already have a criminal record, or are in any form of hot water with the police, because they will take the opportunity to turn your words around and use them against you at the end of the process, which is say 'No Comment'.

I was charged along with my co-defendants, with 'conspiracy to rob persons unknown' and 'possession of offensive weapons' - a knife and CS gas.

After a few days in the police station, I was remanded into custody. The prosecutor was there telling the judge how I had CCTV in my house and how I had just finished doing 25 years for shooting two policemen. That was enough. No bail - lock him up!

We were sent to HMP Wandsworth, and as soon as they put my name on the computer, a big red X came up, telling them that I was a Category A prisoner. That was it - down the block for you, sunshine - you have to go to Belmarsh. Belmarsh. I was there within two days. That's where the horrors really started. An officer that I had left on bad terms with nine months ago was the happiest man alive when he saw me. He came running onto the wing, saying 'I told you you'd be back, I told you you'd be back', and I was like: 'I don't want no trouble, so can we just leave the past. Please.' He said yes. But I knew I was gonna have a run for my money with him about.

The magnitude of my situation hit me hard. I had basically put my whole future and the rest of my life on the line now. I had to run a gauntlet which was not in my favour, if I were to have any chance whatsoever to redeem myself. I started thinking about all the other people who fell into the same trap by coming out, running around and coming straight back in again for life, and I did not want to be one of those people, just another statistic.

The fact that I was in Belmarsh and my co-defendants were still in Wandsworth prison, made it even harder for me to work with them on a defence, because this was a case where everybody needed to be singing from the same hymn-sheet for us to get justice. Therefore, it was only at court appearances that we could talk together.

From the second hearing it became clear that one of my co-defendants, Marlon, had no intention of singing any tune, from any hymn-sheet, for anybody apart from himself.

I managed to get a QC that I was not really entitled to because Queen's Counsel is generally reserved for people on murder charges. Otherwise it is hard to get legal aid, but on this occasion the QC in question, Rajeev Menon, agreed to work for a barrister's fee and this made it possible.

While on remand, I met another inmate that I really liked and viewed as a very intelligent person. We would talk into the night because he was in the cell next door to me; he would go over my case with me and when I told him my defence, he said it made perfect sense.

I was meant to be getting tried at the Old Bailey and we made two appearances there, but then all of a sudden we were moved to Woolwich Crown Court, which has a very bad reputation for low acquittal rates. I knew in my heart that I had to get a not guilty, if I wanted to have any future whatsoever.

Before the trial started, the jury was selected and I was watching the line-up intently. We ended up with two black women, one black man, two senior white women, a young man and then a mixture of middle-aged white men and women, who looked like they came from different class backgrounds. I was looking at them, thinking to myself 'These 12 people hold my future in their hands'. If any of you ever read this book, I thank you from the bottom of my heart and may God bless you until your last days on earth.

The morning the trial was going to start I read the Quran; then I just started to talk to God and I was the sincerest I have ever been. I promised him that if he helped me to get justice and my freedom, I would never put myself in a situation like this again.

In a trial the way it works is the prosecution have their say first, and then the defence. Because I was the number one on the indictment, it meant that I would give my evidence first, after the prosecution had rested their case. My QC and I had already decided that we were throwing in my lot, everything including the kitchen sink, and not holding back about my past, because we knew that the prosecution was banking on us trying to keep it hidden, so that they could railroad us and so I would not be in a position to call them liars, as this would give them the right to bring in my criminal record. Therefore, it was wise for us to do it first so as not to seem dishonest.

The prosecutor's name was Mr Moore - a right whiny self-righteous motherfucker, who thought he was smarter than he really was. So it did not take long for there to be fireworks in the court. We managed to question the armed police's version of events and give them a reality check and then we dropped my record into the arena. So now we were free to talk about the money that got stolen from my house, free to talk about the racial abuse and assault by the armed police, free to tell it as it really was. Mr Moore was not happy about this, so when the time came to go in the witness box, Mr Moore was ready for me. That is until I pointed out a few facts, like the fact that they did not know who was going to get robbed, or if there even was going to be a robbery. They were saying this stuff purely because they knew it could put me away for life. That charge of conspiracy is sometimes worse than being charged for actually doing something.

I was on top of everything and pointed out to Mr Moore that he should work for Sony PlayStation, because he had a good imagination and that I had nothing to hide, as all that really was going on was an insurance fraud, ie somebody was going to claim £300,000 for jewellery that had been stolen in a fake robbery. Mr Moore was like: 'You keep saying you've got nothing to hide and that you're sorry. Were you sorry when you shot the police in the back?' Then he sat down and I just turned around and said to the jury: 'I am sorry about the police. I'm sorry for them and for myself and for my family and the whole thing is and was a sorry situation.'

After me, it was my Moroccan co-d's turn and he said the same as me. My other co-d's situation was a bit different, so all he had to do was account for himself. That left Marlon, who did not wanna sing from the same hymn sheet and who had made a statement in the police station - the only person to do so out of the four of us. I was perfectly entitled and within my rights to tear him a new arse for that, because he was going against all the rules and social norms of the situation, so I instructed my QC to take him to school and my QC just took him to pieces. He had the jury laughing at him and everything. All the while I'm watching the officer in charge of the case and I can see from his body language that he knows he is losing, but is trying to keep a poker face.

After all the evidence was given, Mr Moore, who had not done enough, tried to shore up his case with a long closing speech, stating that even I had had to say it was a robbery. 'Leroy Smith, who does he think he is, ladies and gentlemen, accusing the police of theft and assault?' he said. 'He intimidated his co-defendants.' And then the little racist said that it was no wonder I let my Moroccan co-defendant knock on the front door of the victims, because 'No disrespect, members of the jury, but I wouldn't answer the door to any of the other three, would you?' This was a clear reference to the fact that three of us were black and our Moroccan co-d was very light-skinned and could pass as white.

If you're reading this book, Mr Moore, I hope you are happy in your life, locking up people every day, guilty or innocent.

After the prosecution closing speech, my QC was next; then the barristers for the other three made their speeches and then we had to wait for the jury. They came back after a day and found one of my co-ds not guilty, the one who did not have much to explain. Then they came back with the verdicts for me and the other two.

When we were waiting for the verdicts and I heard 'Not guilty' of conspiracy to rob, the hairs on the back of my neck stood up. I noticed the officer in charge of the case run out of the courthouse, presumably to get on the phone to his boss at Scotland Yard to give him the bad news. It was such an electrifying feeling; the pressure and tension were just rising out of me. When I was walking back down the stairs to the cells, I just screamed out like an animal; words could not come out and it was just like a mad scream and wail all at once.

I got two years' imprisonment to run concurrent to my 25-year sentence, as a result of my co-defendant having a knife on him, not of actually having one myself.

After the trial, I was sent back to Full Sutton prison, in the heart of the dispersal system with all that that entails. But this time being at a complete disadvantage because the whole prison knows you are only there for a short time so you will not really be up for any crazy stuff, like stabbing people up and burning them with hot water, because that would lead to you staying in prison forever, while they could afford themselves that luxury, because they were never getting out, so were free to do whatever they pleased.

Chapter 16

Full Sutton

BBC NEWS 17 February 2014

Three prisoners demanded the release of radical cleric Abu Qatada while threatening to kill a prison guard they had taken hostage, a court has heard.

Feroz Khan, Fuad Awale and David Watson made the demands while holding guard Richard Thompson captive at HMP Full Sutton, near York, in May of last year.

The alleged incident took place four days after soldier Lee Rigby's murder.

Khan and Awale, both 26, and Watson, 27 deny false imprisonment. Khan and Awale also deny making threats to kill.

Khan denies further charges of causing grievous bodily harm to Mr Thompson, relating to allegedly fracturing the guard's cheek, and assault occasioning actual bodily harm against a second officer, Rachel Oxtoby.

A jury at Woolwich Crown Court heard Mr Thompson was captured and held hostage for several hours by the three inmates on 26 May.

'Muslims are fighting back'

Judge Michael Topolski QC told potential jurors that during that time "threats were made to kill the prison officer" and "demands were made for the release of Abu Qatada".

Prosecutor Sally Howes, QC said Mr Thompson was held as part of a "carefully thought out, fully prepared and well planned" operation.

She said it had taken place at a time when relationships between staff at the maximum security jail and some Muslim inmates had become "strained" in the wake of the killing of Fusilier Rigby.

The court heard that two days before the alleged incident Khan and two other inmates had walked out of Friday prayers after the imam offered condolences to the Rigby family.

Ms Howes said Khan had gone on to tell a prison guard "Muslims are fighting back" and "And that's why people are getting killed."
The court heard he said the fight would continue until Sharia law was established in every country.

The trial continues.

I personally know two of the individuals involved in this incident, for which they were accused of hijacking a prison officer and later were found not guilty. One of them is Khan and I can say for a fact that this system is 90% responsible for any radicalisation that is inside that man, because he came to prison for a straightforward murder, involving a bunch of kids from his local area in a street fight. This was a guy who made a very bad but simple mistake by getting into that situation. But he wasn't a bad person, just an everyday young man. However, once the judge sets the tariff for the sentence, it is for the prison service to evaluate you and - if you are willing or trying to make progress – help you to move forward, so you can be released at the earliest possible date, even if it is in 15 years' time. Therefore, they have a moral obligation and duty to make sure that the system – which they pretend is perfect - actually works. But in his case, this did not happen, because his family had money, to the extent that they drove nice cars and visited him and sent him things he was allowed to have, which looked expensive from a prison officer's point of view. So, the prison staff decided, for no other reason apart from that, and the fact that he was born a Muslim, that they would consistently and persistently harass him and make every part of his life a misery. As a result, the prospect of his leaving the high security prison estate where he should never have been held in the first place, all of a sudden became impossible. Then they started making allegation after allegation about him; all this was at the beginning, the first three or four years of his sentence,

I saw him five years or so later and he was a different person. He had resigned himself that the powers-that-be did not and do not wish him any good whatsoever on planet Earth. So he wasn't wasting his time even trying to jump on to a hamster's wheel that rolls on and on to nowhere. His religion is the only thing that no one could ever take from him and he can draw strength from that. When I saw him last in Full Sutton at the time of this incident, he was fine physically.

Earlier on the same day as the incident with the prison officer, in the morning I had a minor altercation with another inmate, and he wanted a way out of the situation. The landings have got cameras on them, so you are under observation 24 hours a day, so he went to the kitchen, filled up a flask of hot water and then walked to my cell door where I was standing and attempted to throw water in my general direction. None of it touched me and as far as I was concerned that was just a publicity stunt, because he knew that we were both going to the block, until they worked out why he had decided to throw water at someone else on camera.

Consequently, I was in the block. When night fell that day there was pandemonium. In the whole history of Full Sutton nobody apart from prison officers has ever spoken on the loudspeaker throughout the whole prison. But these three prisoners spoke for hours, giving their version of their situation as a prisoner, and without asking anyone's permission to do so. The whole prison, black white, pink and purple, listened to the sermon, but whatever each individual's views was on what the men were saying, I can't answer for. What I can say, however, is that if the prison service had not looked at Mr Khan as a Muslim or a person to be viewed with extreme suspicion, I have got no doubt in my mind that he would have been in a Category C prison by now, regularly seeing his family and getting ready for his new future with them, after paying for the actions which originally brought him into prison. If you read this book, my brother, I love you as a person, and you are wise enough to know that every man shall walk this road until the appointed hour.

These were testing times for me, but somehow I managed to keep the order and focus that would eventually lead me back out onto the streets.

I managed to get moved to Belmarsh for my parole hearing and the parole board chairman was competent and realistic and I was granted my parole for the rest of my licence. This is the law, that your licence period is meant to be served within the community, unless there is a reason why you cannot be released, and in my case there was not such a reason.

Chapter 17

On the road today - reality and politics

Prior to my release in May 2014 I was given the same probation officer, who promptly arranged for me to have a police escort upon my actual release from Belmarsh, to my new bail hostel, which this time was in Kilburn.

The hostel had all the same rules and procedures as the first one in 2011, but this one had a rowdier clientele, the majority being young black guys who thought they were badder than they actually were. In reality, most had a lot to learn and I am sure in their own time, they will learn it.

I was in this hostel for about three months, under severe surveillance, courtesy of New Scotland Yard. Once everybody realised that I was indeed a person who had given himself a reality check and I was not going to fall into the many traps and regulations that are laid out for you upon your release, I was discharged from the hostel and left to fend for myself.

I was put in bed-and-breakfast temporary accommodation, which was a total nightmare. I had two single beds pushed together in order to make one double bed and even this did not really work out, because the beds were so cheap that a lot of the middle panels that held them together were missing, so at times if you turned over while in bed you could easily fall through one of the holes onto the floor. This is the truth.

An old Iraqi lady and her son were living on the same floor as me, and all she used to do was walk around saying 'Problem, problem; we have to call the police'. She would say this in response to anything, until I actually had to ask her if she was mad. Why did she feel the need to call the police for everything? She replied 'Problem, problem, call the police', and with that I gave up.

It was at this point that I had to become proactive with different agencies in order to get myself a flat.

In the temporary accommodation there was also a dead skinny Somali sister whose English was so good you might think the queen taught her to speak it. She would go around all day saying things like 'I can't go there, because the ninjas will get me', referring to other Somali sisters who covered their faces. I did not realise at first that she was mad, and for a few weeks she explained to me how the process worked to obtain permanent accommodation, ie a council flat. I do not know how she learned all of this, considering the depths of her personal problems with mental health, but she did and I grabbed the opportunity and registered to bid for a flat. I also wrote to the MP and spoke to anybody in the council that would listen. My strategy eventually paid off and after a year outside, I ended up with a flat that I am very grateful for.

Throughout these times, there were points where money was really hard to come by. People who were in a position to help decided, for whatever reasons, that they were not going to, and some of them did this under bad vibes, as if they did not really wish me well or want me to be able to survive in this new concrete jungle I had come out to. It was totally different from how I was treated in 2011.

There have been times during the last year when the electricity would cut off and I would have to put just one pound on it or on the gas to survive the day and then whatever money I did get I would stretch out as much as possible. It was at these times that I found out who my friends are and this whittled down to a number that you could count on one hand.

It was at this point, that my wonderful partner advised me to write a book. One of my cousins also said to me: 'Your story is a story that people want to hear and it just might do some good, some way or how you can partially redeem yourself.'

To be honest, people had been saying for years 'Why don't you write a book?' 'Why don't you write a book?', but it just did not happen. This time, however, knowing the truth, which is that the past is in the past and it cannot be relived, unless you are willing to risk going back to prison for the rest of your life. At this stage of my life, I can't see anything which would be worth that. Therefore, it was prudent to start thinking of a legitimate way to make a living and to do something, which hopefully will bring knowledge to some people, wisdom to others and understanding to all.

Politics

Politics is a serious thing, which can get you killed and which I do not have any personal power over as an individual; however, I like to observe politics on the world stage, or should I say Western world stage. The knowledge I have acquired has come from 10 years of watching Newsnight every night, and lots of other news stations, so I can crosscheck them and glean what I believe will more likely to be the truth than whatever I am being told on the TV. This is as well as reading some non-mainstream newspapers like Fight Racism! Fight Imperialism, which gets sent to quite a few prisoners in the dispersal system, and which I received through most of my sentence.

Now after all these years of observing, I would say I've got a good understanding of what is really going on around me. Life today is worlds apart from the 1990s and the gap between rich and poor is so wide it will never ever get closed again and just gets wider. In order to survive, countries gel together; that includes companies and big corporations in order to hold more sway and to achieve their objectives whatever they may be.

As a black man and ex-prisoner, who age is getting the better of, politics is a bittersweet pill. I like observing it, but I do not like watching people on TV claiming to be my representative, lying and lying about the history of this country and its part in slavery. It feels nice to me if I see a young black man in a nice car, or with a nice job or higher education, because I know how far we are coming from. Then at other times I look at the ironies of life - for example, because of slavery and the money that it generated, David Cameron would be born into a family, generations later, that could afford to send him to Eton, from where he could become a Prime Minister. And it doesn't stop; it just keeps trickling down, and in his case, it's a proven fact that a large portion of his family's wealth came from slavery. Even after slavery was abolished, they were so disgruntled that they refuse to release the slaves unless the government paid them for them. This is the nature of his family. Those slaves, 120 of them to be exact, were just tossed out with no more than the clothes on their backs and they had to survive, generation after generation, and they are in our society, just like Mr Cameron, but the only difference is that, more than likely, they will be uneducated and living in an underprivileged environment. These are all raw facts that people don't wish to look at because it does not suit their purpose.

I have also noted that the majority of the world's poor are people of colour. This negative in itself can be used as a positive, if applied positively. Therefore, if you are living in England and you are poor, we would have power in the political process just by joining together on the platform of being poor, through social media or whatever platform.

This would include every colour, and then, just like that, instead of being one person, you are 20 million votes. In a country of 60 million that is a lot of votes; enough to make any politician or government acknowledge you and your wishes, which like most people, are the same.

The whole political arena is slanted in favour of the rich. In essence that's what capitalism is about. The only time the have-nots have a chance to do something is on voting day. The other three years, 364 days belongs to them and they will use it to make data and surveys, all along threading you into a system which is viewing you as a number, a system that gives you just enough to survive, always wanting more, an unforgiving system that rolls round and round to nowhere. Surely that can't be someone's idea of a good life.

But in saying all this, we always have to remember too, that the powers-that-be have no intention of ever relinquishing power. A perfect example of their capabilities and deceitful nature is the Hillsborough disaster - 96 people unlawfully killed at a football match and the police decided to blame the victims for their own deaths. It has taken the families and friends of the victims 27 years to achieve justice and for the powers that be to backpedal and start telling the truth or accepting the truth. So there you go. That's the world we live in.

Total respect also to Black Lives Matter and their peaceful demonstrations - that's the way to apply yourself in this unjust world.

Looking forward

I have done so much wrong in my life and I have lived far longer than most people who have lived the way I have lived. All I wish to do now is give something back to society, because I know the truth having walked this road myself.

Like remembering the days of having £10,000 pocket money every day and flying all around the world, having everybody say 'yes' to you just because they're scared of you going on the phone and telling someone in another country to do acts of violence to people and it's done. All of these things make you feel important and powerful, but it is all short lived.

Post codes. Young black kids are actually dying over them when in reality the post code and the area do not belong to them. They do not own anything in or around any post code. This is how ridiculous life has become. More to the point, Babylon is happy when young black men who are meant to be the future turn all dysfunctional and fight amongst each other. All of these things keep you at the bottom of every pile that exists. There is no future in it; therefore, if you are already involved, and you've got money around you, I would strongly advise you to put it into some legal enterprise for your future.

The prison system is getting worse by the day and it is a nightmare I would not wish on my worst enemy. Please take my word for it, I beg of you, because if you go there you will never be the same again.

As for me, the most I can hope for is to be in a position to go to schools and talk to young people, and if that leads to changing even one I will feel better about myself. So this is more a personal journey, but one that is so unusual it would be for the greater good to share it with the world. Be all you can be don't get tricked and become a victim. We are the people and this book is for the people, so share this on Facebook and Instagram or whatever media network you work with, so that as many people as possible get to read this book.

And so I have finally come to the end of this process. England has left the EU, David Cameron is resigning, but the cycle of life continues. My life now centres around my dog Casper and my inner circle of close friends. Whatever the future holds, I hope it will be something which can help the youth because they are the future.

My black is beautiful, wonderful, powerful, mystical; my black is beautiful.

Leroy Smith

With thanks to Rachel, Eric, Justin, Nicki, Ryan, Leon, James, Jason, Garcia, Kevin, Tanya, Richmond, Ainsley, Simon, Jane and Nia and everyone else who has helped or inspired me in the writing of this book.

RIP Mikie Sprang

slain by an unknown gunman, 22 July 1997

Afterwords

To my beautiful mother, strong black woman who was brutally taken away from me by a scumbag at a time when a big investigation was not necessary because both parties were black and in those days when the police service was 100 times more institutionally racist than they are now: Not a day goes past when I don't think about you. When I see some child with his or her mother and wonder what it would be like if it was me; I see the joy and interaction between them and feel happy for them, but this is tinged with great sadness for me. I will never forget being two years old and seeing you in that box with the glass top, still and dead, and I could not quite understand and started crying.

And to the prison officers in HMP Long Lartin who thought there would be nothing more enjoyable or nicer than in the morning in 2004, telling me that my grand-dad - my next-of-kin - had died. They did this by coming to my cell with big smirks on their faces as if they had just got the best news in the world. Then one of them said 'your grand-dad's dead' and slammed the door in my face. To you unprofessional and uneducated, sadistic form of person, death comes to us all rich or poor. Therefore, when your turn comes, or when people you love leave this earth, I hope the people around you show more compassion and are not of the same breed as yourselves. And to you, governor Sidney, who said to me that I could go to the funeral of my beautiful grandfather - who worked for this country like a slave since the day he was born without ever stealing a penny, until he was old and bed-ridden - and your sense of humour was to tell me I could go to the funeral when you knew full well you were not going to let me go. When the appointed time came, I found out that I wasn't going anywhere. You must be retired now if you are still alive. I hope you look into yourself and reflect and ask yourself what your evil actions gained you. Whatever you all think of me, my mother loved me.

My daughter's view

What you gave me

I remember the day my father was sentenced to 25 years. I was seven years old and it was broadcast on the 6 o clock ITV news, I remember seeing him being taken away from the court in a prison van and a reporter describing how the heinous Leroy Smith was now where he belonged behind bars. I sat gripped to the news report staring at the familiar police mug shot. Even though I was only seven, embarrassment filled my every being. Sarah from school's father was a fire man and Caroline's father was a business man, mine was a cop shooting drug seller. After the news report I ran from the living room in floods of tears. I don't think my mother had meant to expose me to the news report, but it's not like you could have hidden my father's crimes away; they were very public, an open sore I've tried to get away from my whole life. We had neighbours knock on our door to show my mother the latest press cutting as the case of the cop shooter unravelled.

Before my father was arrested he would turn up randomly at my mother's house, they were never a proper couple and so the ideal I had of a 1950s style pin-up mum and dad wasn't my fate. Even though I was small I always felt there was something about him that was different. I never bonded with my father as he was very unapproachable. As I grew up, and after my father was sentenced, I learned more about him (things I wish my mother had kept to herself). My father's trial and imprisonment had led my mother to have a nervous breakdown. Letters he sent her, with scribbles of coffins he was 'going' to put her in, would land on our doorstep almost monthly and I know she felt spooked by these. Oddly I never felt scared of my father, even though I knew what he was capable of. I just felt very let down and abandoned. I spent my days daydreaming about being the daughter of some famous couple, or just even Mr and Mrs Normal, anyone but my parents. My mother had turned from someone who adored me into someone who constantly told me how much I reminded her of the gangster. I now became accountable for the hurt Leroy Smith had put her through.

Leroy (as I called him for many years) was in prison, but I was in a prison of his making (I felt) with a woman who despised me and, in the same breath, loved my every fibre. My volatile relationship with my mother, coupled with her mental health, meant I was placed in foster care aged 15.

Growing up I think I've lied to almost every friend I've

had about my father and his role in my life. I once told an employer my father was an artist in the 1970s, I went to great pains to express how fantastic and creative my father was. Other times he's been a business man or an accountant (you can't get more stable than an accountant) anything but who he is, the cop shooting drug seller and Cat A prisoner. For the first time in my life I can proudly say my father is an author. Now I'm an adult and a mother to an adorable baby the 1990s seems so far away. I've made peace with myself, by letting go of what I cannot change and doing everything in my power to be the best mother ever. There's so much I could write but it's not my book. My relationship with my parents is estranged but I wish them both well and, like I previously said, by writing this book my father has finally done something I can be proud of and my child can reflect on without stigma or shame.

New era

'Don't move! Don't move! I've got you motherfucker and I'm going to blow your head off!'

Wow here we are in 2020 and I am living a new life that not even my wildest imagination would have really believed would turn into reality. All because of hard work and ultimately this book Out of the Box.

After the publishing of the book in 2016, doors started to open. Slowly at first, with invites to small youth clubs; then I start getting paid talks, and going to different places, like City University, and then I was invited to Oxford University. I started getting opportunities to get into big newspapers, with articles in The Guardian, Independent and Times, both talking about my own journey, and commenting on developments in crime and justice. I appeared in a documentary made by the Open University about prison and punishment, and on radio, including Radio 4 and National Prisoner Radio.

Being in The Guardian gave me the opportunity to be

involved in the documentary Gun Number 6, which ultimately won a BAFTA. I both appeared in the documentary and was involved in finding other people to take part. Five former gunmen talked about our own lives and experiences, as well as acting in the re-enactment scenes depicting true incidents of gun crime. It was amazing an experience being on set, and seeing the different sides of the production, not to mention going to the BAFTA and Grierson Award ceremonies, and to do Q&A sessions at Sheffield and Aldeburgh documentary festivals.

I have also done work inside prisons. I worked for six months at HMP The Mount, and did Black History Month presentations there and at Ranby and Featherstone prisons. I have done countless talks now to schools and youth clubs and have looked into the eyes of more than 1,000 young people, and spoken to them and told them the truth about life as I see it; this always strikes a chord with them, because they can relate to what I am saying. Nothing is rehearsed; it is all real natural talk from my heart. In 2019 I did two stints of paid mentoring for teenage boys who had lost their way – very challenging but rewarding work.

After the book was published, somehow one of the officers I had shot read it, and the book touched him, and he decided to reach out to me with the view of forgiving me for the dreadful thing that I did. My close friend, who had been in the background all the time advising me, agreed to come with me to the train station to meet James the officer that I shot all those years ago. It was a scary situation and I was scared because I was the one that done the wrong. At the train station I looked into his eyes and apologised and then held out my hand. He shook my hand and then we had a cup of coffee and a down-to-earth talk. It was very emotional powerful experience and I was totally humbled that this man could forgive me for actually shooting him. It was more than I believe I could do.

Since then we have been communicating by email and somewhere along the line the BBC heard the story and approached us and we decided to agree to an interview, which was carried out a few weeks later. This was an amazing success with hearts and minds all over the country it is still on I-Player. It also led to a lot of radio interviews after that main interview, and even an invitation to New Scotland Yard.

So, there you go, hard work can pay off, and I have made a complete U-turn in my life. I drive a nice car and I haven't got anybody, ie police, stalking me and I'm free to live my life and do whatever I can for others, especially young people because they are the future and that is what counts. My story is one of redemption and it is so powerful that we are working with a scriptwriter to make it into a mini-series for TV, telling my story and that of James Seymour, as we grow up and live our lives until the day we collide together on that dreadful night, and in the aftermath when I go to prison and James recuperates, until we meet again many years later.

I am continuing to do public speaking, both individually and on panels – and these days often on Zoom, for universities; schools, pupil referral units, youth clubs, bookshops, and public meetings. I have my own charity Out of the Box Community Effort, which in 2019 was awarded an Antoin Akpom Achievements Foundation award for Community Contribution.

You can do it!

Do right for yourself in life, blessings!

Leroy Smith

The Other Side

by James Seymour

My upbringing could not more opposite than that of Leroy's, I was brought up in a small town in Kent where crime was rare, and it was like the town just shut down at 9pm every day.

My family were Strict and Particular Baptists; the 10 commandments were endorsed very literally, I had no TV or radio. Discipline was almost Victorian. The downside to this is unlike my siblings I rebelled. I didn't like being told and forced as to how and what I should think and behave; I just wanted to be myself.

I did, however, learn to respect others and put them first before me. I have respect for all religions but I cannot understand when a particular belief says theirs is the right way. That causes tension and hatred as we've seen throughout the world over the years and in the UK too. Live and let live and respect each other's beliefs.

I loved sport, especially football and cricket, but was not allowed to play on Sundays so I lost interest. At 16 years old,

I discovered girls which also didn't help with my sporting abilities and desires to excel. 1976 was a year I distinctly remember, watching the West Indies cricket team on my friend's TV absolutely destroy England. They were my heroes, all of them, just so dedicated, fearless, hungry to win.... Sir Viv Richards......just incredible. Even now I love watching YouTube clips of his laid back demeanour but just so talented. When I played, I wore a maroon cap like Sir Viv, just wishing I could play like him and be him. Pele was one of my footballing heroes, first played for the Brazil national team aged just 16....awesome.

I went to a grammar school but I wasted my education as part of my rebellion, I was once told Maths and English were most the important qualifications to possess, so that's all I worked at and passed at O Level grade. I also passed at woodwork which I still enjoy. All I wanted to do was work, get some money, drive a car and have a girlfriend. I left school at 16 and got the first job I could, working in a plastic moulding factory nearby doing unskilled labour. But it paid quite well so I bought myself a car and taught myself to drive on a cousin's farm. My love of driving had started and 40 years later I still get a buzz out of it especially at work. Those working five years were invaluable experience of achieving some life skills before becoming a police officer. I'm not a supporter of people who go to university and then join the police although it was and still is encouraged. Life skills and experience are far more desirable.

My life was still being controlled at home and I got to the stage where I had to leave, I applied for Kent Police but they didn't want me, but the Met did, so aged 21 I went to Hendon police training centre for 20 weeks. I struggled so much with the studying law and procedures and I was extremely shy in those days. I was, however, determined to pass as I couldn't go home and the term 'pain is temporary, to quit is forever' served me throughout that time and my life.

I got posted to South Norwood and lived at Tooting section house at the back of the police station. This was for single officers who didn't live in London, and had basic facilities. Days off, it was just party, party, party, and I loved it for four years.

But there was a downside to joining the Met, realising that policing was stressful, difficult, you were hated by some people from all communities and you could never do the right thing. At times you felt like giving up and letting the public just get on with it; this feeling is so relevant in today's society. The public actually need to sit back and appreciate what police officers actually do. It's not all about arresting people and stop and search; there is so much more to it. But as an officer you keep going, hence my phrase just mentioned.

These were new experiences and sometimes difficult to adjust to. Most police officers are proud of what they do, it's said most people deal with three or four traumatic incidents in their life, Police officers might do that in a week, and so if their patience sometimes isn't what it could be, there may well be a reason for it.

I was regularly posted to Crystal Palace football matches and luckily on a few games I was posted to the players' car park, where I met another hero of mine, Ian Wright. There was always some banter between us, but there was a mutual respect, and I still admire him for his skills both as a player and a football pundit. That was a real positive for me; however as a 21-year-old in 1984, dealing with a suicide at Thornton Heath railway station, in which a man had been decapitated by a train, was my first introduction to the gruesome side of policing. Having to take fingerprints from his corpse to try and identify him. (No DNA in those days and limited technology). Could you have done that at that age? Three years later, I was 24-years-old, trying to save a baby's life that had been stabbed by his mother suffering post-natal depression, living in conditions not fit for human life, and not her fault.

The standard of accommodation was a shock, let alone the circumstances of being there. Sometimes I feel people should look at what they've got and just be grateful; we all want better. We tried so hard, but he died in our hands, I felt guilty like I had failed. I've never forgotten that sense of disappointment but my colleague and I did the best we could. Sometimes you need convincing you couldn't do more because you care. The mother was not charged due to her mental condition but given support. Years later I often wonder what happened to her.

In 1991, I dealt with a stabbing at a private house in South Norwood SE25, whereby a Rastafarian drug dealer had been slashed across the stomach with a machete. The mother and sister were not supporters of the police, but we arrived before the ambulance. This man's injuries were serious and he was clearly going to die soon. There was a desperate look of 'please do something' on the mother and sister's faces, so my colleague gave CPR whilst I tried to hold the contents of his stomach together and inside his body. It was an impossible task but after a few minutes the ambulance crew arrived and did their best; however he did not survive. I remember the mother and sister thanking us for our efforts; we had made a positive impression on them. The same feelings return; you feel that you've failed, let a fellow human down, yet deep inside you know you couldn't do more. It's a strange feeling. I know at that time there were lots of police officers who wouldn't have tried to help him survive, but just how would that look to the family?

It was realising this man was part of a family, whatever his history and background. It was police helping the black community. It's strange, but in 2004, I tried to resuscitate a white male trapped in a car after a crash in Bellingham with both legs broken. Turned out he had over 1kg of cocaine in the car but little did that matter. Somebody's son, somebody's brother, or even some child's father.

Following the Lord Scarman reports after the 1981 riots it was recommended that police officers be transferred from their stations after five or six years to prevent the temptation of corruption and supporting unprofessional behaviour and over-familiarisation. I fully agreed with this and was offered a place at Brixton which I accepted. I transferred in 1992. However, whilst waiting my transfer date, I would like to mention an incident whereby the black community helped police. There were two crews who had been assigned to an emergency call in Addiscombe, Croydon, myself being one of them. The frequent abandoned 999 call with a disturbance heard in the background. This type of call you had no idea what you were attending; the control room would try and ring back the number, but usually it was still engaged and off the hook. The other crew arrived first; probably less than a minute, when one of them called out for urgent assistance as they had been stabbed. As a police officer, it is the worst sound and words you can hear, and literally makes the hair stand up on your neck. We ran up the stairs into the flat whereby a woman, probably in her early 50s, was screaming. Inside I saw a black man restraining another black man against a wall in the lounge, assisted by one of the stabbed officers, with the use of a large round dining table.

The male was holding a large carving knife, trying to stab what turned out to be his brother and the officer who had been stabbed already. The other officer was on the floor seriously injured. Eventually the four of us, including the brother overcame this man and he was restrained. He was not a bad person; he was suffering from serious mental illness, although at the time I might not have said that. One of the stabbed officers, who managed to help detain the man, had been stabbed in the sternum with such force it bent the blade of the knife. One centimetre to the left and it would have been fatal. Both made a full recovery and bravely returned to frontline duties. Total respect to them and that influenced me to do the same later in my career.

So I went to Brixton with a lot of experience in the time I had been in the Met and same type of calls, lots of domestic incidents, condensed street crime in a smaller area, but what was different was the open drug dealing on the streets in Atlantic Road, Loughborough Road and Landor Road in particular. It was just so blatant and many police operations took place, some of which I took part in, and made very little impact. The other difference was increased aggression towards police. It didn't really bother me, but I was conscious that I needed to be totally professional with what I said and how I dealt with the public; feelings from the early 1980s had clearly run deep and been passed onto the next generation.

A couple of years went by. I was popular and respected by the team I worked with and I had two young daughters. Financially, life was a struggle with a mortgage and young family and I worked as much overtime as I could. The night of our shooting, 9 March 1994, was no different, looking for an easy arrest for possession of drugs, a quick caution in custody - but our plans were soon to change.

I won't go into all details but simply a motorbike with rider and pillion had gone through a red traffic light at Atlantic Road and Coldharbour Lane. By the time the lights changed the two on the bike were now walking, still with crash helmets on from Rushcroft Road into Coldharbour Lane. The body language of them just wasn't right; they were startled by us, but we had no other reason to speak to them. We found the motorbike on a pavement and the number plate check revealed no current keeper. Suspicions grew. We then went around the block a couple of times. We spotted them, as they did us, aware and watching each other. There was just something going on; it's been said that streetwise police officers develop a sixth sense, a sense of survival or that something isn't how it should be. We saw them at the bike and stopped to speak to them, just another stop in the street. They were told of what we had seen, to take their crash helmets off and that they would be searched for drugs.

Without warning the atmosphere just changed; it had started as a compliant stop, no attitude from either side, but it was strangely tense now and there was no going back. As I went to search the rider he dropped something on the floor I believed to crack cocaine. I was aware of my colleague struggling with the pillion, Leroy Smith. They were on the floor when I saw the black handgun and then heard the shot, I heard the scream of my colleague and saw him grab his leg. There was just adrenalin pounding through my body, I didn't want to believe this was happening; it was just a nightmare, and so often in trauma life just goes into slow motion.

Leroy shouted at me to 'Fuck off', urgent desperate tone in his voice. He was clearly out of his comfort zone too, but as I turned to look for cover, the next round hit me, like a red hot needle through my flesh, passing over the top of my kidney and ripping an exit wound in my side. But the physical pain was nothing compared to the feeling of total helplessness. I had seen a colleague shot. I had nothing to protect myself from a gunman. I was helpless for both of us. I couldn't do anything to protect or help us.

I took refuge beside a white van and felt the blood pouring from my side. Training kicks in: back injury, don't move but control bleeding, so I squeezed three fingers into my own body, my bleeding side. to stop the flow. I was determined, saying to myself 'I'm not going to die here'. I remember Leroy and his colleague shouting at each other, just thinking 'why don't they just leave?' We had called for help on our radios; as another shot was fired, I just didn't want anyone else to turn up and get injured. It was only by reading Leroy's book that I found out the delay was due to an anti-theft device on the motorbike.

The first officer to get to us nearly ran me over, as I was in the road. Sadly Floody, who was like a brother to me, was killed in a motorbike accident a couple of years later. This event in my life was probably what triggered my PTSD. Simon and I were pall-bearers at his funeral, on the hottest day of the year in August 1997, and he wasn't exactly slim, that coffin was so heavy, but I just know he was looking down on us with a big grin on his face. I still miss you mate.

We were taken by ambulance to Kings College Hospital; both of us had surgery. I was released from hospital after four days, but had to attend daily for two weeks to have the wound cleaned and dressed. My colleague was in hospital for three weeks and then received physiotherapy at the army rehab centre at Headley Court in Surrey. It's strange but at that time he was the only person there with a gunshot injury; how much did that change after Iraq and

Afghanistan. We decided to return to work together after six months; we were both ready to take up the challenge and to police Brixton again, although we were offered any posting in the Met. We had to prove to ourselves that we could still work in one of the toughest environments in London. Trust me that took courage beyond what words can describe.

Throughout the early days I never had any hatred towards Leroy, but there was a real sense of relief when he was arrested in Connecticut USA; it was to me justice was about to begin. I was bitter that he had shot us when he could have just fired a warning shot, but as police officers are taught when you get faced with confrontation and mental stress, it's fight, flight or freeze. Leroy didn't want to go to prison, so he went for the first instinct. He has admitted to me recently that's all he needed to do, but that was his split second decision. I have really tried to understand that. Hindsight is great, and applies to all of us, what we would like to change from the past. The incident was not really discussed with my family; sometimes it's easier not to ask if you're not sure what the reaction will be from that person. Or you might not agree with the answers. Some people just simply don't know what to say.

After returning to work after the shooting – this would be summer 1995 - I was driving a marked police car in Coldharbour Lane. I don't know who my operator was but it was a hot summer's day and absolutely heaving with people. There had been tensions between the black community and police; I can't remember why, but you could sense it in the atmosphere. Whilst stuck in traffic with the window open, a young black lad, probably about 18-years-old, wearing a string vest in Jamaican colours, came over to the car on my side. I can still remember I had negative thoughts like 'here we go again' or 'what grief is he going to give me?', but I was so wrong. In front of the crowds he handed me an ice cold can of Jamaican ginger beer (which I still love) and said ' that's for you bro I respect you'. I was very humble but asked 'what about my mate?', meaning the operator, and he just replied, 'no respect, I don't know him but you're different'. He just went and disappeared in the crowd, obviously he had recognised me from media coverage of the shooting. That young lad doesn't know what good he did. I've kept that for 25 years and I'll never forget it, we seem to think the worst of people when actually there's more positive than negative.

When I returned to work at Brixton after the shooting I had a chat with Janet Hills, now the top person in the Met Black Police Association, who was a PC on my team, asking me had it affected my views working there and towards the black community. I can clearly remember her saying to me she hoped I wouldn't think all black people were bad, I know she was concerned but it made an impact on me. I remember saying to her I was better than that and of course not. We had a big hug and I kissed her on the right cheek. I recently emailed Janet; she doesn't remember our conversation but was so pleased I never forgot it and it meant so much to me. I believe she asked me as I was a friend and wouldn't want that to happen. She is an incredible person in the role she has and I have nothing but admiration for her.

The trial of Leroy and his accomplice took place in Court Number 1 at the Old Bailey. It was an unusual layout of a court and steeped in historic trials over the years. It was stressful as my five-year-old daughter was recovering from meningitis, having been hours from dying. In Court Number 2 was the trial of three white men accused of murdering Derek Robertson. my friend both at work and outside of it. He was the best sergeant I worked with, such a lovely, family committed man and great police officer. He led by example.

I went to the trial on most days, and when Leroy was

convicted he formed his fingers in the shape of a gun, faced us and fired one more pretend shot. At the time I didn't hate him for doing that but I felt degraded and didn't deserve it; however over the years I realised he was facing 25 years in prison, I had my freedom so what did he have to lose. The entire jury returned to see what he was sentenced to, I shook hands with them after, they were from all different communities and backgrounds and it was good to know that they cared about me and my colleague.

I saw a counsellor who was excellent; some have the qualifications but lack experience, but she was different. She changed careers and we lost touch, a real shame. It was not: 'Sit on the bean bag and download your thoughts, when did you first experience trauma in your life?' It was: 'Remember you have been through experiences that even the Commissioner of Police hasn't, so that makes you a higher rank than them; just drop subtle reminders now and again so they don't forget. You are special. Be positive you survived.' Great words of advice, Janet; thank you so much for what you did. I was visited in hospital by the Commissioner Lord Condon, and the following weeks at home by a Chief Inspector from Brixton several times. To be honest not much really came out of it and that officer was clearly out of his depth communicating with me after my experience. Rank but no experience. There was at this time no real evidence I was suffering effects of trauma as there was lots of media coverage and interest from friends. I was having issues at home though.

As time went by I still had no hatred. I had simply been in the wrong place at the wrong time, or the right place at the right time, so no one else public or police got hurt; you can look at it from both ways. I had been lucky to survive and knew my injuries could have been so much worse, but not lucky to have experienced the trauma. I had extreme guilt that my colleague had been more severely injured than me with a fractured thigh bone. I felt guilt that I should have done more to help, although in reality I couldn't have, but it caused that moment of helplessness to keep continuing.

With all the incidents I had talked about earlier (and there were more) I suffered PTSD - Post Traumatic Stress Disorder. It's evil, wicked, like falling into a dark hole that has no bottom. You are desperate to just find something to cling onto, some hope, to have some control on your life; you can't see any positives, nightmares often involving family. Suicide is considered, and I was no different. It is more frequent than many police officers or public would believe. The loneliness I cannot describe. I turned to alcohol, which just made things worse, although temporary relief until you wake up.

If you get diagnosed with a serious illness like cancer, people know and can offer sympathy and support, but with this you appear normal outside; if you tell them you're suffering from a trauma related anxiety they generally wouldn't know what to say. But inside it is eating away at you. I tried to talk to people close to me, but through no fault of their own, they simply didn't understand what I was going through. My warning to emergency workers is it might not kick in until years after the event or a build-up of traumatic events. You must talk and release, but you also need someone who is an active listener. It is not weakness, and to deny it or believe it will go away with time, trust me it won't, it will only get worse. Other signs are hyper activity, or picking arguments with loved ones to make you feel better, as you feel so low inside, and you feel the guilt later because you started it, so then you become even lower. I'm ashamed to say I've been guilty of that. Being ultra sensitive is another as you feel so low. I felt so alone that no one understood what I was going through.

I continued to work throughout this time, I had many friends whose sense of humour kept me going, but they didn't know how I felt inside. It was all a front. My first marriage fell apart partly because of the PTSD (as my second did as well) and it effecting my home life, so I felt I had to keep going at work, but other incidents just made things worse. My girls also kept me going, the time I spent with them was and still is invaluable; I will always be in their debt. I'm glad to say dealing with mental health in general, not just for emergency services and armed forces, has moved on and help is far more available and professional now. There still is further improvement needed though. It is a huge issue for police officers and I sometimes feel they are unfairly expected to be specialists in this matter. So much of what they deal with is related. I would love to help emergency workers suffering from trauma; I have a life full of experience and although no paper qualifications. Op Hampshire are interested in me helping assaulted officers. I am a firm believer that assaulting any emergency worker should be treated as a hate crime. Far too many nurses and doctors in Accident and Emergency wards get assaulted daily; it has gone on for years and they need protecting.

I met someone who had served in the Royal Marines at Kosovo; we immediately recognised there were hidden demons and talked for ages. Although in totally different circumstances, he opened up to me, trusted me and told me some absolute horrors he had witnessed. He hadn't even told his colleagues. He was a broken man. It put me in my place and I realised that the traumas I had experienced just weren't what he had been through. There is a saying there's always someone worse off than you, and meeting him made that come true. It put everything in my life into perspective. Thanks Ben, opening up to me put me on the road to recovery.

Returning to the scene of a traumatic incident is invaluable to dealing and coping with what happened, and unlike Ben I was able to do that. I would advise to everyone if you can do that it will be for the better. It's tough to do so but the outcome is so beneficial. I would like to say thank you to Leroy for putting me in touch with copsalive, an organisation from the USA who try and look out for police officers involved in trauma. They look at experience not qualifications.

I carried on working on the emergency response teams at Penge and then Lewisham, and I would like to think I was a role model for young officers, both from an officer safety side but in speaking and dealing with public from all communities. I then joined Hendon driving school as an instructor, although still a police officer; I was still deployed for policing public order events such as sporting functions, Notting Hill Carnival and New Year's Eve celebrations.

I had a slight relapse of PTSD in 2007 when, performing a demonstration drive in Finchley Road north London, I drove into an armed robbery. Members of the public directed us to a side street where the suspects had gone; we had no information they were armed. A Golf GTI made off in front of us and I gave chase. Game on! They entered a cul-de-sac and the two occupants ran off, with the three students and I giving chase. From about 25 yards, one produced a handgun and fired two rounds at us from under his left armpit. Luckily no-one was hit, but did that shake me up again? Both got arrested and convicted. All the cash was recovered.

I had just taken up running due to being overweight and I became addicted; that was my release from trauma and if you've never tried it, exercise is just mind clearing, mental strength building. So tough to start but here I am 10 marathons and 26 half marathons later! Remember the saying about pain being temporary? I had the pleasure of meeting Dame Kelly Holmes on a few occasions as she used to own a café near my home. She is a lovely lady, gave me running tips and I told her she had made me proud to be British with her sporting achievements.

After 30 years distinguished service I retired as an officer, commended for bravery on 10 occasions, which now hang in my spare bedroom and I look at with pride regularly. Two were for the firearms incidents both already mentioned, six for knife crime, but one I'm especially proud of is for helping a 13-year-old Sri Lankan girl, trapped by her head in the rear door of an overturned car in Catford. Her family could speak very little English; all the windows were smashed, petrol was leaking heavily and the car could explode at any time. You have to take risks in life, especially as a police officer, so I crawled inside the car, cutting myself to pieces on broken glass and broken trim, my colleague Matt pulling open the rear door with all his strength to free the girls head, he was at the same risk as me. We managed to pull her out and I'm glad to say she made a full recovery eventually. I was told at the time by high ranking police and fire officers we shouldn't have done that. All I can say is you've not been in that position in life. I didn't care what background the girl came from; she was scared and injured and her family distraught, and we were both prepared to pay the ultimate price to save her.

As the years went by I grew to accept what had happened in my life and could live with it; however I always wanted to meet Leroy, to see if he really was as ruthless and uncaring as he was made out to be. I wanted to know more about life in prison: was it really a sentence or an easy way out for criminals? I was told by Victim Support who kept in touch with me (thank you Beverley for your caring support and professionalism) that Leroy had written a book. A crew of students I was training heard the conversation with her, and they bought a copy of Out of the Box as a token of appreciation at the end of the course. They each wrote some comments in the front saying I was an inspiration for all officers. It made me feel good and I hope I still am. I read Out of the Box and then read it again, I liked the honesty and maybe not all the content, but I decided to email the publisher to send a note of praise to Leroy and to stay on the correct side of the law. And that's how our amazing journey started.

I was emailed back by Leroy who couldn't believe what I had said; he was extremely emotional. The emails became regular. At first there was distrust from both sides, and understandably so, but as time developed so did our trust. We talked about meeting; there was originally apprehension but we fixed a date of 25 April 2018 at Charing Cross Station. From my point of view, there were lots of public around and CCTV. I had told a couple of friends I worked with but they never followed it up.

I walked up the escalator from the underground; my heart

was pounding as I just didn't know what to expect. I looked around several times hoping my emails hadn't been seen and I was followed by surveillance officers for whatever reason. I got off the escalator and looked around, didn't see Leroy, but then again didn't know exactly what he looked like. Then I was aware of someone walking towards me from the ticket office direction. It was Leroy, accompanied by a longstanding female friend.

We shook hands, the same hand that had held the gun and pulled the trigger in 1994. I felt a sense of peace, massive pride that I was doing this. I didn't feel I was better than Leroy; I knew I had had a better life and opportunities than him, and that wasn't really his fault. He said he was sorry and I told him it was time to move forward with our lives. I bought him a coffee and we sat and chatted. One of the first subjects was what good had come out of the tragic death of Stephen Lawrence for police investigations, crime scene management, and honesty and self-criticism within the police service. I don't know if he was surprised by my direct approach to this, but we agreed on so much. I shook hands with him again when we parted, I remember on the train home thinking I can't believe what I've just done. It took massive courage from me, it took massive courage for Leroy, he thought I might be seeking revenge, but I know he soon realised I wasn't like that.

So our friendship grew, emails, WhatsApp messages, video clips. We chatted about our love of dogs; Leroy even told me if he had a dog in his life in his youth he wouldn't have got involved in crime. He absolutely loves and worships Casper, who is one lucky dog to be cared for like Leroy does. I've met Casper and the relationship between him and Leroy is superb, Casper is in great condition. During the recent Covid-19 pandemic we contacted each other weekly to check up on each other's health. It was genuine from both sides.

I know this bonding will not be accepted by many people, friends and family, but all I want is to make a difference to one person's life, which I know has already happened. I want Leroy to know he has my support for helping youngsters stay out of prison and away from crime. I hope before someone disrespects police officers they may just think of what I've written and change their opinion. Police run towards danger or drive as fast and safe as they can towards danger, and not away from it. That could be a terrorist incident, or someone armed with a knife or gun. They are human although that's sometimes forgotten. The terrorist that killed PC Keith Palmer was immediately given emergency life support from an armed response officer, not there just for his firearms but his additional skills of dealing with ballistic injuries. His armoury on this occasion was a first aid kit .That takes a unique type of person and he is not alone.

Think of positives before negatives. I recently met Leroy at the scene of the shooting. I had been back there several times including during the 2011 riots. It had always been rewarding for me in accepting what happened and having met Leroy there was tough for him as it was his first time returning to Brixton. I found it tough too, meeting someone who had nearly killed me at the place it happened was brave but I'm so glad it's been achieved. Personally for Leroy, as I've said, I never hated you, but forgiveness wasn't easy and took time. It's made me feel so good inside, I feel peace, my head is as pure as spring water, and I know your life has changed dramatically after our bonding. I have given you a wonderful opportunity in your life to turn bad into good or even better. Grab that opportunity with both hands, and don't let go. Our journey is powerful and just beginning.

To those that have read my chapter, I wish you the best in life, I'm no hero just a simple, honest, caring, professional man with a heart the size of the world. As Gandhi once said 'forgiveness is the attribute of the strong' and that describes how I feel now...strong. Take care, stay safe.

Printed in Great Britain
by Amazon

75911553R00112